Democracy, Pluralism and Conflict

Democracy, Pluralism and Conflict

EDITED BY
M.N. KARNA

RAWAT PUBLICATIONS
Jaipur • New Delhi • Bangalore • Mumbai • Hyderabad

ISBN 81-316-0019-X

Published by
Prem Rawat for **Rawat Publications**
Satyam Apts., Sector 3, Jawahar Nagar, Jaipur 302 004 (India)
Phone: 0141 265 1748 / 7006 Fax: 0141 265 1748
E-mail: info@rawatbooks.com
Website: www.rawatbooks.com

New Delhi Office
4858/24, Ansari Road, Daryaganj, New Delhi 110 002
Phone: 011-23263290

Also at Bangalore, Mumbai and Hyderabad

Typeset by Rawat Computers, Jaipur
Printed at Chaman Enterprises, New Delhi

Contents

Preface

The essays on democracy, pluralism and conflict included in this volume were originally presented at a national seminar organized by the Department of Sociology, North-Eastern Hill University, Shillong in May 2002 under the UGC Special Assistance Programme. A seminar is usually an exercise in sober exchange of academic inputs and is structured so as to create an aura of dispassionate analysis, specially if it happens to be on a theme like democracy and pluralism. But, the logic of histories we have been forced to live in have somehow taken away the comfortable world of such sober exchanges. The times are such in the country today that even off the cuff platitudes on democracy is bound to be relevant. Our aim in putting these essays together in a collection is to bring the issues of democracy and pluralism to the central focus in the study of social change in India. We seek to address the problem that has both theoretical significance and substantial policy implication. It is particularly so in the backdrop of emerging threat to the very survival of secular democratic fabric in the country.

It will be obvious from the contents of the essays that although all the authors are sociologists, they look beyond the narrower parameters of their discipline. They have ventured into fresh areas to comprehensively analyse the issues involved in ideals of democracy and pluralism. In this sense, there is a thematic continuity in all these essays.

We are thankful to a number of individuals and institutions for their support in the publication of this volume. The authorities of North-Eastern Hill University and the Indian Council of Social Science Research provided financial assistance for the seminar which is gratefully acknowledged. We owe special thanks to the contributors, who not only presented their papers at the seminar but also revised them for publication in this volume.

M.N. Karna

Introduction

Democracy is essentially a thing of faith before it is a matter of fact. It has neither a shared meaning nor there is a consensus on the elements that give it a shape. Does democracy refer to individual freedom or merely a majority rule? How to judge a country as democratic or to assess its progress towards democratic structures? Should all-embracing institutions exist in a society to claim the designation of democracy? Obviously, no simple answers exist. In fact, the attempt of arriving at an unambiguous meaning of democracy is often treated as an academic wrangle to confuse the issue. We all know which nations or states are democratic and which are not and for most of us there seem to be no need to enter into such a pointless argument. However, what we aim to highlight here is that the term 'democracy' cannot be applied in a commonsensical manner to grasp the democratic ideal and the structure of the contemporary world.

Democracy in substance is defined in terms of two basic principles, viz., popular control over collective decision-making and equality of rights in accomplishment of that control. The degree and extent of realization of these principles give shape to a democratic system. In this sense democracy does not belong only to the sphere of the state or government but it is also relevant to any kind of association, which is based on the process of collective decision-making. Thus, while analysing the idea and structure of democracy, both the issues of structure of governance and democratic values in other social domains of the state have to be kept in mind.

Conventionally, we characterize a state democratic if its government is answerable to the people through elections to public office based on the canon of universal adult franchise and where civil and political rights are statutorily guaranteed. However, no state in practice fully realizes the ideals of people's control over public affairs and political equality. Even when universal adult franchise is achieved or popular elections assume central place in the political system, democracy is far from being fully realized. This understanding is primarily based on the premise that the goals for which common people want democracy are yet to be achieved in most of the countries. The inherent logic in the principle of democracy in this sense necessarily points towards the development of democracy in production and distribution, social and cultural spheres as all these are decisive areas of people's life. We thus maintain that democracy is still 'unfinished' task on the agenda of modern society and the struggle for deepening it continues.

The long history of democracy as a form of state or government has not reduced the value of its historical and practical significance. Its relevance as a competing ideology of the present time survives because the reasons why democracy is valued and justified are as fresh as they were at the initial stage of its imagination. Equality of citizenship, guarantee of basic freedom, necessity of meeting popular needs, the reality of diversity and plurality within society are concerns that can be ensured only in a democratic setting. "Everyone to count for one and none more than one", said the English legal theorist Jeremy Bentham in his attack on the aristocratic view that some people's lives were intrinsically more valuable than others. The precept of equality requires that not only needs and interests of people should be looked into by the government but their opinions should also equally count. The democratic system stresses participation in the affairs of the society by the individual member on the basis of his/her personal selfhood as a human being regardless of his/her abilities, rank, status or possessions. Democracy has thus evolved as an instrument to challenge privileges based on status and ascriptive attributes. In other words, the system of representative self-government derives its power from the people. It is in this context that equality and freedom find a place in democratic theory. The 'equal say' of all individuals in arriving at collective decisions provides the rationale for government by the people. However, the mechanism through which this goal can be achieved is the principle of majority rule. The latter represents the most feasible plan of action for arriving at decisions when there is no unanimity among people on various issues of crucial importance.

Related to the principle of equality is the ideal of social justice. Reducing inequalities and augmenting equality of opportunity are the two crucial aspects of social justice. By according equal political rights to all categories of people, constitutional democracy acts as the means to achieve social justice. However, political equality alone cannot accomplish justice for every section of society. It provides equal rights but not the equal opportunity to exercise those rights. Under the condition, a democratic society has an obligation to take care of the disadvantaged and deprived categories of people. Rawls, a philosopher of distributive justice, appropriately argues that social justice is, and must be, the central agenda of liberal democracy.[1] "To single out the least advantaged and maximise their long term prospects consistent with the liberties of equal citizenship is, in his view, the ethos of democratic society."

The basic issue involved in the problem of distributive justice is the difference in life-chances that are available to the people. The basic structure of society favours certain groups and collectivities over others. These inequalities affect their whole life prospects. The distributive shares based on the principle of justice depend on the fundamental system of rights and duties ingrained in a society. Moreover, the idea of justice as fairness is the most rational basis for a common public understanding of the issue of constitutional liberty. Justice requires the elimination of institutionalized discrimination and the creation of a balanced system within its structure.

Equality before law and of opportunity does not guarantee equality of life-chances. Institutionalized social hierarchy and distinction between groups on account of vast disparities in wealth and resources restrict life-chances of socially deprived groups. The latter more often than not are victims of a long history of exploitation, oppression and discrimination. They have for generations been denied adequate opportunities for growth and development. Naturally, most members of all these groups are poor and suffer from ill-health, high rate of infant mortality and shortened life expectancy. The absence of proper education, health care and emotional stimulus leads to stunted growth of their character, ambition and self-confidence. A deep sense of injustice and discrimination haunts them all their life. It is against the background of people's social backwardness that the concern for social justice is back on the agenda of democratic project.

The benignancy of a society is judged by the degree of protection it provides to its disadvantaged and less 'gifted' members. In a democratic society reasonable restrictions are placed on the acquisitiveness of its more advanced members and special safeguards provided to its weaker and more vulnerable sections. These issues are fundamental to any scheme of social justice and their neglect makes a society insensitive and uncaring. Elaborating on the notion of social justice as a right in a democratic society, Justice K. Subba Rao writes:

> ... the right to social justice may be defined as the right of the weak, aged, destitude, poor, women, children and other underprivileged persons, to the protection of the state against the ruthless competition of life. It seeks to give the necessary adventitious aids to the underprivileged so that they may have the equal opportunity with the more advanced in the race of life. It is a bundle of rights; in one sense it is carved of other rights; in another sense it is a preserver of other rights. It is the balancing wheel between haves and have nots.[2]

In this sense, when applied to a system of institutions, justice requires the elimination of arbitrary social distinctions. In a democratic society, a proper balance has to be established between the principle of equal opportunity and the doctrine of special opportunity to eliminate the existing inequality. To achieve the goal of social justice, the policy of positive discrimination has to be brought into the agenda of the state.

Another important aspect that assumes crucial significance in democratic ideal is the idea of cultural diversity. It is argued that no discussion of the definition and measurement of democracy today can be satisfactory unless it is grounded in and informed by a full appreciation of the inescapable reality of cultural pluralism.[3] Liberal theory of democracy has been lukewarm towards the question of diversity. The assertion of equality in democratic state structure does not always take into account the cultural differences that exist among the people. Modern nation-states are characterized by multi-cultural and multi-national settings. The ideal of formal equality is simply committed to individual equality. It is not sensitive towards cultural identity of the people. While articulating this principle, differences of social status, religion, language, race and ways of life are invariably ignored. By treating unequals equally, 'marginalized' groups are placed in a disadvantageous position. Equality may end up emphasising the assimilation of marginalized communities into the culture of dominant group. Such an understanding of equality not only ignores cultural diversity but also sets aside cultural differences between communities and groups and attempts to bring them under the uniform laws. The civil laws and patterns of dominant culture thus push marginalized and minority communities towards the condition of deprivation and discrimination. The demand for uniform civil code in India, frequently raised by various social and political groups, comes in handy to illustrate the point.

Cultural diversity and pluralism must be incorporated into the democratic theory and practice. It means all culturally distinct groups must be treated equally and no discrimination has to be allowed in terms of differences in religion and race, caste and creed, or language and lifestyles. Cultural diversity is treasured because it deepens our understanding of culture and enables us to enrich our way of life by borrowing whatever is valuable in others and can be integrated in our own. Since it is a valuable 'collective good', it gives individuals a sense of rootedness and self-confidence. Cultural diversity admires and shows consideration for different cultures and promotes a dialogue between them. The value of cultural diversity should therefore be recognized and cultural heterogeneity preserved. When diversity is recognized and becomes essential element of the policy of a state, it requires that minorities should be protected from deliberate and latent discrimination in various domains of life. Furthermore, it may require some restrictions on the freedom of some groups. For example, the protection of identity of a smaller tribal community, say of India's northeast, may require curbing of rights of landownership to the outsiders and the free entry of people to the region from outside. Such restrictions are justified if they are directed towards protection of cultural diversity.

Moreover, the term 'cultural diversity' is also applied here to take note of the reality of pluralism. Pluralism includes both cultural and political pluralisms. The identity of a group in cultural terms is as important as its mobilization for gaining political power. In other words, every group and collectivity, while preserving its cultural identity, lives side by side with different groups in states and competes for sharing power in political domain. Contextually, therefore, different sets of institutional arrangements are needed in multicultural societies for democratic governance.

These fundamental concerns of democracy, viz., equality, social justice and pluralism, as discussed above, are further linked with the idea of secularism. Secularism safeguards the interests of individuals and groups in religiously diversified countries. Democracy and secularism do not only match but they are to be paired to acquire a place in a democratic system. Although imprecise use of the term 'secularism', both in literature and in political discourse, has created enough confusion but its substance cannot be overlooked whatever way it is elucidated.

Historically, wherever democracy has been achieved through struggle, separation of state and church has been ingrained in it. Even, in Europe, it represented the political dimension of a process, which had emerged with the Protestant reformation. The supremacy of church over theological, juridical, economic and administrative spheres of society was challenged during the period of Renaissance and French Enlightenment. This struggle was equally involved in demolishing the hold of feudal lords and church nexus on the civil society. The growth of social norms around modern rationality has to be understood against this background. Modernity and secularism are not merely ideological precepts of philosophers but are also the outcome of the struggles of the masses. Secularism vindicates the basic democratic rights of equality, justice and freedom from discrimination and oppression. As such, advocacy for secularism is advocacy for the cause of people, irrespective of caste, class, sex and religion.

The thrust of our argument may be briefly summed up in these words. Democracy has emerged as a total philosophy in contemporary world. All those values and structures which 'revolution' intends to establish have now become essential elements of democracy. Human rights, gender equity, social justice, protection of minorities, fulfilment of people's need, rule of law are all issues of democracy. They can be achieved through the democratic process. Thus, the challenge today is to elevate the revolutionary character of democracy.

* * *

Indian democracy is a conundrum. While it is glorified as the largest democracy in the world by some, others condemn it as fake and likely to falter soon. Such extremely contradictory representations are primarily witnessed because the Indian democracy does not fit into any given models of democracy. Most of the stable democracies today have industrialized and capitalist economies unlike India which continues to be essentially agrarian with a highly hierarchical social order. Survival of constitutional government, regular elections, freedom of expression, free press and an independent judiciary existing within a hierarchical social structural setting seem incredible and unheard of in the history of democracy. While many countries may claim to be democratic, their political institutions obviously display the fragility and vulnerability of democratic arrangements. The contemporary Europe itself testifies that democracy is a difficult form of government to establish and sustain. The experiences of fascism, Nazism and totalitarianism nearly attempted to eradicate democracy altogether. One should not forget that democracy has evolved through intensive social and political struggles and if not effectively defended it may peter out easily. The history of democracies in a large number of post-colonial states in Africa, Asia and Latin America amply lends credence to such an assertion.

How should democracy be assessed in India? What should be the parameters to judge its successes and failures? Has it proved successful in meeting the challenges for which it was established? Attempts have been made to measure modern democracy both in qualitative and quantitative terms. While qualitative parameters include the principles of popular control and political equality, the extent of participation and contestation constitutes quantitative indicators. Although these sets of parameters fall under different domains but operationally they are intimately linked and are combined to assess existing democracies.

Indian democracy is situated in its republican constitution. Some observers highlight its glorious past and attempt to analyse its history against this backdrop. Our argument is different. It was not the consciousness of the glories goneby that determined the nature of political democracy in India but it was the goal of meeting the challenges of the newly independent country that brought a republican constitution to create a democratic setting. The newly independent country with perplexing religious, linguistic, regional and caste diversities amidst problems of illiteracy, poverty and all round economic and social backwardness called for development and modernization within a reasonable period of time. The adoption of republican constitution and establishment of parliamentary system of government was actually the beginning of a struggle to sustain India as an independent state based on the democratic ideals of secularism, economic equality, political freedom and social justice.

The establishment of popular democratic government, based on universal adult suffrage, free and fair elections, guaranteed fundamental rights and an independent judiciary, provides the strong foundation on which the democratic system rests in India. The effective participation of the people in political process is ensured by the regular conduct of elections at scheduled intervals with increasing voter turnout. It has not only reinforced the system but has also helped in further consolidating the democratic institutions. The rate and extent of voter turnout in general elections has demolished the prevailing assumption that educational and economic advancement is an essential pre-requisite of a genuine democracy. The existing trend is just the reverse when it is witnessed that voter apathy is largely confined to the middle class section of India's population compared to the disadvantaged groups of every social and regional setting.

The wider involvement of the mass of people in political activities in general and the marginalized groups and communities in particular is further discernible in increasing number of people who are coming forward to contest elections, irrespective of caste, gender and religion. Over and above, its range and reach has expanded after the introduction of various tiers of statutory panchayats since the 73rd and 74th amendments in the Indian Constitution. The new dispensation, which ensured reservation of seats and posts for women, members of the scheduled castes, the scheduled tribes and other backward classes, has opened up additional avenues for participation in the decision-making process. It is expected that a more democratic panchayat in the long run will not only ensure people-oriented development but will also be more accountable to people. Once the disadvantaged sections participate in the deliberations and decision-making process, they will not only demand effective participation but also the kind of development they want. Thus changes brought about by the panchayati raj institutions promise to strengthen the process of democratic decentralization of the Indian state and, if given the chance, it will provide grounds for political mobilization of those sections hitherto excluded from participating in the local planning and decision-making processes.

It is however necessary to acknowledge that the electoral process is losing out on credibility since mid-80s because of the ominous trends emerging in the conduct of free and fair elections. Unprecedented cases of booth capturing, the increasing number of election-related killings, the incidence of malpractices, and the uncontrolled use of money and mafia power witnessed during the last few general elections are eating into the vitals of the electoral system. The entry of confirmed criminals into state legislatures representing various political parties seems to spoil some of the grandeur and dignity inherent in the democratic image of India. The criminalization of politics continues to gain political legitimacy its unlawfulness notwithstanding. The menacing trends in the electoral practices are however not a threat to the very survival of parliamentary democracy because it is still localized and manageable. In reality, these drifts are expression of expanding nature of democratic participation. The locus of power in rural areas is substantially shifting from the hands of upper caste landed gentry to the dominant middle caste self-cultivating owners. While the limited numerical strength of the former has restricted its widening base, the latter has successfully mobilized its fold for enlargement of political support. Under these conditions, the political space created by democratic institutions at different levels is being replenished by fair or foul means. A close look at the nature of malpractices in general elections apparently shows that no candidate (or faction) can favourably manage them unless he/she has a strong base in the area of his/her operations. To put it differently, the increasing number of election-related killings and violence in most of the cases is the result of inter-caste antagonism and election is just a pretext to perpetuate it.

It has rightly been indicated that besides elections other avenues of political participation have also emerged. The democratic formation has given voice to the deprived castes and communities. The increased political assertion of dalits, tribals and members of the middle range castes has assumed the shape of organized movements. They have been launched in the context of social and economic backwardness and have acquired democratic character because demands are articulated and expressed in terms of political rights and entitlements. Some movements have no doubt adopted the extra-parliamentary path but they are essentially struggles for democratic rights since they have emerged basically as a response to the violation of civil liberties and human rights.

The continuing demands for formation of new states within the Indian Union, clamour for preservation of ethnic and cultural identities in the northeastern region, protests against development-induced displacements are all directed against the Indian State. Likewise, dalits and tribals have reduced their ascriptive attributes to economic choices and cultural practices into political symbols. The primordialist identity is used for instrumentalist goals, as the former becomes political resource for the concerned groups. The mobilization of such consciousness for political action is a significant development. Notwithstanding the regional and sectional character of these movements, a culture of movements has engulfed the country as a whole. It is difficult to locate a group or a community, which is not in a ferment. It is safe to suggest here that socio-political movements have made Indian democracy more 'inclusive' by extending its reach and expanse. As democracy relies upon debates, persuasion and negotiated compromise, the inclusion of more and more people, irrespective of caste, creed and gender, leads to strengthening of democratic edifice by creating space for expressing differences of opinions and interests.

Another dimension of democratic institutions that requires to be discussed is the party system and leadership. Political parties constitute an essential element of the institutional arrangement in a democratic system. Individual electors choose governments through the exercise of their voting rights in free and fair elections. The choice of candidates is offered by the organized political parties. Thus, the consolidation of democracy and its growing strength lies in the development of a sound party system and the availability of effective and efficient leadership.

How does the Indian balance sheet in this respect look like? The system has been characterized by one party dominance, which Rajni Kothari described as the 'Congress system'. Although the Congress party provided a great deal of internal flexibility and a long period of stable democratic functioning but eventually it led to a centralized bureaucratic structure, making the system unresponsive to the people's aspirations and needs. It also manifested regards for India's diversity during the early decades after independence and gained wider legitimacy. But, in the subsequent phases, fast erosion of the democratic values pushed the party under the control of the 'political managers' who had least respect for justice, fairness and impartiality in public life. It is difficult to pinpoint with certainty the factors behind such faults and distortions in the Congress system. Nonetheless, we may direct our attention to two major factors in this context. They are weak institutionalization of developmental ideology and declining performance of parliamentary and party institutions. The conversion of developmental ideology into programmes failed to achieve its objectives. Hence, the path of development, instead of producing a just and equitable society, led to growing marginalization of the poor, increasing inequality and discontent among almost every section of the population. Moreover, erosion of parliamentary and party institutions manifested in centralization of authority, all-pervasive corruption and growing nexus between party bosses and industrial-urban mafia. It also resulted in diminishing secular and modernizing beliefs creating space for communal forces to emerge. The subsequent developments amply show the increasing influence of emotive appeals of a communal kind.

The state of affairs of other political parties is also not altogether different. Parties of the left variety are involved in resolving their own internal contradictions. The socialists of all shades and opinions forming parts of the so-called 'Janata Parivar' are struggling to preserve their left-over identity by shaking hands either with the Bhartiya Janata Party or the Congress. The regional parties, on the other hand, are busy in arousing ethnic and regional sentiments to consolidate their support base to justify their relevance. Accordingly, an obvious shift in political astuteness of these parties from socially progressive national outlook to retrograde localized ethnic slant is not only visible but also growing stronger day by day.

A few words now on the trajectory of secularism in India, which has been extremely complex. The term 'secular' is used here in a pluralistic sense and not in the sense which expresses indifference to religion. A mono-religious society can develop a political process exclusively independent of church. But, a multi-religious society draws strength from its pluralism. The Indian social setting, characterized by religious diversity, has to follow this path.

Given the context, a vocal section in India challenges secularism primarily on the ground of it being an alien concept having no relevance to a highly religious ambience of the society. All those who champion and campaign for secularism are therefore considered pseudo-secular. They strongly argue that the existing rationalist notion of secularism, based on criticisms of organized religions in India, results in pampering the minorities. The strong communal prejudice involved in this argument is too obvious and hardly requires elaboration. It makes majoritarianism its major plank and leads to the breakdown of consensus that had emerged in the country on account of the increased democratic consciousness among the masses.

As against this extreme position, the term 'secular' has also been used in two different ways. Of these, the most popular meaning says that the state will accord equal respect to all religions while the second suggests that the state will keep equal distance from all religions. These meanings obviously suggest that no religion be given preference to others by the state. Every individual is free to follow his/her religion without encroaching upon other's right to do so. Of course, such a simple and uninvolved meaning of secularism does not attack religion and keeps it in play enhancing religiosity which helps in projecting religious identities leading to the increase in social distance between different religious communities. Under the circumstances, state itself may go religious if political exigencies so demand. However, such a possibility will always be there even if further refinement is brought in the Indian meaning of secularism.

Our contention is that a strong appeal for democracy and democratic institutions has taken a firm root in the country and have their expressions in a model which includes two ideological inputs: one of secularism suited to a multi-religious and highly plural social order and the other of economic development based on the canon of equity. Nonetheless, we witness a visible mismatch between the practice of democracy and the pluralism of society. The heightened communal frenzy, inter-caste tension and persisting unrest in different regions of the country amply bear out this mismatch. Communalism has emerged as a major political force and it is clearly a sign of willingness of some people to accept secular democratic politics. The steady erosion of both democratic institutions and the values, which were cherished in the early decades of independence, has threatened the future of democratic and secular India. However, a ray of hope is still there. The awakening, mobilization and ideological assertion of the people at the various reaches of social hierarchy are indeed deepening whatever remains of the democratic institutional fabric of the polity. So long as religion remains a social fact, it cannot be easily wished away. Secularization of religion is a contradiction in terms but secularization of polity is a possibility, which can be achieved through struggles. The struggles for spreading and consolidating secular values require that certain elements of religious values are appreciated, some others are tolerated while a fight is initiated against some.

Against this background, issues such as cultural diversity and democracy, democracy and cultural identity, secularism and communalism and multiculturalism and conflict have been discussed in the essays that follow.

Notes

1. J. Rawls, *A Theory of Justice*, Oxford University Press, London, 1972 and 'Distributive Justice' in P. Laslett and W.G. Runciman (eds.), *Philosophy, Politics and Society*, Third Series, Basil Blackwell, Oxford, 1967 [experted in Gurpreet Mahajan (ed.), *Democracy, Difference and Social Justice*, OUP, Delhi, 1998, pp. 255-282].
2. Justice K. Subba Rao, *Social Justice and Law*, National, New Delhi.
3. See Bhikhu Parekh, 'Cultural Diversity and Liberal Democracy' in D. Beetham (ed.), *Defining and Measuring Democracy*, Sage Publications, London, 1995.

1

Pluralism, Democracy and Conflict

Situating the Indian Republic

T.K. OOMMEN

What I propose to do in this paper is to attempt a conceptual analysis of the notions of pluralism and democracy and to locate the factors which cause conflict in their co-existence. This exercise is undertaken with special reference to Indian 'society' widely certified as culturally diverse.

I

To begin with, it is necessary to recognize that there are two types of pluralism: cultural and political. The intellectual ancestries are readily traceable to J.S. Furnivall and Alexis de-Tocqueville, respectively. Those who follow Furnivall are principally social and cultural anthropologists and are designated here as *cultural pluralists.* The Tocquevillean line is pursued largely by political scientists and political sociologists who may be labelled as *political pluralists.*

The conceptualization of pluralism is tempered by two prominent factors: the property of the empirical situations in which the researches are undertaken and the intellectual, ideological and disciplinary orientations of the researchers. And yet, we need to reconceptualize the notion of pluralism not only because of the inherent ambiguities in the prevailing conceptualizations but also because of their inadequacy to cope with the empirical situations prevailing in India.

The classic description of plural society by Furnivall (and he did not talk about pluralism), based on the colonial situations he analysed, reads:

> Each group holds by its own religion, its own culture, its own ideas and ways. As individuals, they meet but only in the market place... There is a plural society, with different sections of the community living side by side, but separately within the same political unit. Even in the economic sphere there is a division of labour on racial lines (1948: 308).

That is, in Furnivall's plural society, the co-existence of the different segments, usually of racial collectivities, one native and the other alien, is not voluntary but brought about through the force imposed by the colonial power from outside. Further, given this lack of 'integration', plural societies are utterly unsuited for the emergence of nationalism and hence democracy. "Nationalism, within a plural society, is itself a disruptive force, tending to shatter and not consolidate its social order" (Furnivall, 1939: 468). By implication, only in societies that have been voluntarily constituted and are homogeneous, can democracy be institutionalized and nurtured. Similarly, Van den Berge concludes after an elaborate theoretical discussion: "I believe that pluralism is intrinsically associated with conflict and relative lack of consensus and integration" (1971: 79). However, such a position is not sustainable in the light of available empirical evidence. The most 'successful' democracy in the world, the United States of America, is not a voluntarily constituted polity if one takes into account the manner in which the original inhabitants of the US territory and the Blacks in the anti-bellum south were incorporated. The Union of Indian States, the largest democracy in the world, is characterized by stupendous cultural diversity.

If Furnivall's conceptualization of plural society was anchored to the empirical situation of tropical colonial multiracial societies, subsequent analysts like Smith (1965), Despres (1967) and Van den Berge (1983: 238-52) refined the notion and extended it to the empirical context such as slave and multiracial societies, both colonial and post-colonial. In contrast, the Tocquevillean conceptualization of pluralism is based on an entirely different type of empirical situation that grew out of a multiplicity of collectivities competing in the political arena through the instrumentality of parties and associations, institutions and mobilizations. The typical cases that represent such situations are capitalist liberal democracies of the UK with its multinational and migrant populations, and the USA which is poly-ethnic and multi-racial.

Tocqueville (1956), having observed the persisting turmoil in France, the country of his birth, and the land of the great revolution, was eager to locate the sources of the stable and successful democracy that obtained in the US. He found that there existed a number of 'secondary powers', that is, voluntary associations, and these associations along with the autonomy of local authorities (e.g., municipalities) served to prevent the authoritarianism of the central state and helped to stabilize democracy. Thus, voluntary associations are recognized as countervailing powers which sustain political pluralism in democratic societies.

Political pluralists argue that voluntary associations are instruments that sustains democracy; and these associations are formed on the basis of a wide variety of factors including race, religion, caste, region and the like. The US, the most 'successful democracy' in the world, is hailed as a country of joiners, and the American propensity to form voluntary associations is universally acclaimed (see, for example, Bryce, 1910; Myrdal, 1944; Hsu, 1963). Students of community power, who have dealt with the relationship between structural differentiation and dispersion of power in communities, have also argued that political pluralism is conductive to democracy (see, for instance, Simpson and Simpson, 1964). Similarly, Rogers argues that "the structural differentiation and increased complexity and heterogeneity that accompany industrialization contribute to a pluralistic power structure" (1964: 402). Finally, Dahl (1961: 85) refers to the dispersion of political resources in New Haven in the wake of industrialization and the consequent dispersed inequalities and the emergence of specialized leadership resulting in a pluralistic power structure.

Theorists such as Van den Berge (1971: 67-81) refer to cultural pluralism as the conflict model and to political pluralism as the equilibrium model. The essential source of conflict in the first type—the culturally plural society—is located in the fact that a demographic, racial and cultural minority dominates the majority in every aspect of life. This domination is made possible through their economic and technological superiority. This situation necessarily breeds conflict between the two parties and the resolution of conflict is possible only by doing away with its very source, namely, the domination of the majority by the minority. Viewed historically, however, a large number of such societies have continued for a long time as 'stable' societies, the dominated majority rarely revolting against the dominant minority either because the value of self-governance was not internalized by it or because it did not have the requisite striking power.

On the other hand, it is not true that societies grouped under the equilibrium model—the democratic plural societies—did not have any conflict. Indeed, the thesis of political pluralism which propounded the idea of integration being achieved through multiple affiliation of individuals to a variety of institutions and associations almost entirely ignored the racial minorities, particularly the black populations of these societies. Consequently, conflict, which is almost endemic in these societies, has been ignored. In fact, conflict is more visible in the democratic plural societies than in the despotic plural ones. Thus, conflict and equilibrium are common to both types of 'plural' societies. Therefore, to label these societies in terms of one of these features is inadequate, indeed, misleading.

In the light of these considerations I suggest that we need to distinguish between the two types of societies based on the *quality* of equilibrium which obtains in them. The culturally plural societies are characterized by *coercive equilibrium* and the politically plural societies are informed of *consensual equilibrium*. Admittedly, the real challenge faced by culturally plural societies is to transform their equilibrium from a coercive to consensual one and that of the politically plural societies is to sustain the prevailing consensual equilibrium.

Three general conclusions emerge from the discussion so far. First, the pronouncements regarding the relationship between pluralism and democracy are diametrically opposite. For cultural pluralists, pluralism destabilized the social order and is antithetical to the very ethos of democracy. By implication, they plumb for homogeneity for sustaining democracy. For political pluralists, pluralism is the essence of democracy. Understandably, social heterogeneity is the natural soil on which authentic democracy should survive and prosper. Second, neither cultural nor political pluralists have addressed the all-important issue of institutionalized inter-group inequality, an inherent feature of hierarchical societies such as India. Third, they have not adequately addressed the complex issues of conflicts in societies such as India which combines cultural diversity and political pluralism.

In the light of these points I want to make the following suggestions: First, we must clearly distinguish between four types of societies—stratified, heterogeneous, hierarchical and plural—based on the nature of the elements that constitute them, their internal social milieu. Second, the distinction between plural society and pluralism should be clearly maintained. Indeed, the route through which plural societies can become democratic is to accept the value of pluralism.

Third, the effort to homogenise societies should be abandoned, as it is antithetical to the spirit of both democracy and pluralism. Fourth, diversity/heterogeneity is a social fact, and pluralism is positive value orientation to that social fact.

All societies are stratified on the basis of age, gender and class. However, if a society's population is drawn from the same race, religion and/or linguistic group, it could be designated as *homogeneous*. Conversely, multi-racial, multi-religious, and poly-ethnic societies may be referred to as *heterogeneous* societies. In this type of society, there is a possibility of inequality becoming a formal feature based on race (e.g., South Africa, until recently) or caste (e.g., India, before 1947), which also renders them hierarchical societies. That is, heterogeneous societies with institutionalized inequality are hierarchical. A heterogeneous society need not however be hierarchical as racially and/or culturally diverse groups in the polity may have formal socio-economic equality.

In the cases of stratified, heterogeneous and hierarchical societies, however, the internality of none of the constituent elements is questioned. Thus, the American 'Negro', the Indian 'untouchable' and the Greek 'slave' were all accepted as essential and useful internal elements although equality was not granted to them. In contrast, the internality of one or another segment in a plural society is questioned, that is, plural society is polarized between insiders and outsiders (see, Oommen 1990: 43-66; 2002). Sometimes, the insiders may be marginalized (e.g., the First Nations in the New World) and the outsiders became dominant and sometimes the outsiders may be marginalized and deprived of their rights (e.g., Indians in Fiji, or guest workers in Western Europe). It is of signal importance to note that the first three types of societies are not either/or but additive types. That is, culturally diverse societies are also stratified. Hierarchical societies are stratified and heterogeneous, but plural societies are stratified and heterogeneous although they may or may not be hierarchical. However, they have one or more segments whose internality to the society is questioned. Democracy engenders conflicts in all these types of societies but the number and nature of sources vary; they are minimum and less complicated in homogeneous societies and maximum and more complex in culturally diverse plural societies.

II

Democracy is a term in much wider circulation than pluralism and yet it is not without ambiguity. It is formed through a combination of two Greek words *demos* (populace) and *kratos* (power), meaning people's power; the Indian equivalent being *lokniti*. Both in Greece and in India direct democracy of the people obtained for millennia at the grassroots level; in the former through town meetings and in the latter through gram sabhas. But these direct democracies were imperfect in that in Greek city states only patricians were full-fledged participants; the plebians had access to these meetings but scarcely participated and the slaves were totally excluded from them. Similarly, in Indian villages, the full-fledged participants were only the twice-born caste Hindus; the Shudras, broadly coterminus with today's Other Backward Classes (OBCs), had only limited participation and the Dalits, the ex-untouchables were completely denied participation. At any rate direct democracy is not a feasible project at higher, that is, macro levels. Thus, when one talks of democracy, the reference is to representative democracy.

Two competing models of representative democracies emerged in the twentieth century. The people's democracies of socialist countries provided basic economic security to all citizens in the polity but often denied political freedom to them. The one-party democracies provided representation to citizens not through an electoral arena in which different political parties with dithering ideologies competed and emerged successful; two or more candidates from the same party canvassed support and the more acceptable candidate to the electorate won. Through special provisions for representation to various social segments—women, youth, labour etc. —the different social categories also got their representation. But, with the collapse of the socialist countries, the multi-party system of capitalist societies remains the only form of representative democracy. This system has gradually emerged in the West and subsequently spread to the rest of the world.

Democracy, as a value and as an institution, emerged largely in the twentieth century. In 1900, there were only 25 'democratic' countries accounting for 12 per cent of the world's population. These countries practised restricted democracy in that they gave voting rights only to property-owning males. By 1950 there were 22 electoral democracies, which permitted universal adult franchise, accounting for 31 per cent and 21 countries with restricted democratic practices accounting for 12 per cent of world's population. However, 120 out of the 192 existing countries, accounting for 58 per cent of the world's population, had electoral democracies by 2000. Of these, liberal democracies, that is, countries which represented basic human rights and the rule of law, are only 85 accounting for just 38 per cent of world population. Thus, it can be said that authentic democracy, which acknowledges the basic value of human rights, is not as widespread a political arrangement as is usually believed.

A democratic polity is a collectivity of citizens in which they are endowed with certain entitlements the content of which are essentially three—civil, political and social. These rights emerged gradually in the eighteenth, nineteenth and twentieth centuries respectively (Marshall, 1965). Civil rights consist of liberty of person, freedom of speech, thought and faith, the right to own property, the right to conclude valid contracts and the right to justice. Political rights are mainly the right of franchise and the right of access to public office. Social rights, widely viewed as the crowning glory of citizenship, are actually economic in content (Giddens, 1985: 206-9). These consist of the right to a modicum of economic welfare and social security, to a full share of the social heritage and to live the life of a civilized being according to the standards prevailing in society. That is, citizens of democratic polities are entitled to dignity and self-respect.

Although citizenship is the kernel of democracy, the contents of citizenship vary vastly even between the United Kingdom, 'the first democratic nation' and the United States of America, 'the most successful democratic country' in the world. This comparison is particularly pertinent for the present analysis as the UK is multinational (consisting of English, Scottish, Welsh and Irish) and pluri-ethnic (consisting of migrants from all over the world including Asia and Africa) and the USA is poly-ethnic and multi-cultural.

Americans rarely speak of social citizenship because it implies rights and entitlements embedded in a contract, and it is viewed as a device to extend charity wrapped up in institutional welfare benefits (Fraser and Gorden, 1994: 90-107). Welfare is stigmatized, but work is sacralized; the public domain is demonized, but the private is sanctified. Unemployment is viewed as a private predilection and not as a manifestation of social policy or economic pathology. In contrast, civil citizenship is highly valued. The hero of civil society, created by civil rights, is the property-owning individual; civil society is exemplified by 'possessive individualism', to recall the seductive phrase of Macpherson (1974).

The robbing of social citizenship of its contractual character and viewing it as charity has several consequences. First, the beneficiary becomes a mere recipient of charity with no entitlements—a situation that is morally degrading. Second, the giver of charity assumes instant superiority and accumulates moral merit, the concern being the giver's entry into the other world and not the receiver's physical survival in this world. Third, since the giver and receiver are strangers, the recipient cannot *demand* charity but can only solicit it. And, the cultural mythology of civil citizenship stands in a tense, often obstructing relationship to social citizenship. This is nowhere more true than in the US, where the dominant understanding of civil citizenship remains strongly infected by the notions of 'contract' and 'independence', while social provision has been constructed to connote 'charity' and 'dependence' (Fraser and Gorden, 1994: 104).

The consequence of this juxtaposition of social and civil citizenship in terms of charity and contract is manifested in the widespread belief in the USA that the opportunity for economic betterment is widely available, that social mobility is determined by the individual's efforts, and that, therefore, economic inequality is fair (Klugel and Smith, 1986: 37). Further, the feeling that the recipients of welfare exaggerate their needs, cheat the state and avoid work is widespread. That is, Americans are far more concerned about the duties or social obligations of the poor, particularly those who receive welfare support than about their rights: ... "it is the moral fabric of individuals, not the social and economic structure of society, that is taken to be the root of the problem" (Wilson, 1994: 53).

An empirical analysis, attempted by Conover and his colleagues (1990: 1-33), confirms the differing emphases with regard to citizenship rights between the USA and the UK; American respondents focus on civil rights, whereas British respondents focus on social rights. With regard to citizens' duties, the Americans focus on political responsibility, but the British responses "contained relatively more communitarian elements". The central elements in the identity of citizenship in the USA are freedom and individualism; in the UK these are a sense of belonging to the land, a shared heritage, and a national identity. That is, the conceptions of citizenship vary drastically between the UK and the USA. It is important to recall here that these two 'nations'—the 'first nation' and the 'first new nation' of the world—are widely believed to have common values and institutions; the latter is regarded as a replica of the former. I suggest that the motives for their differences should be traced to the fact that they are drawn from different contexts, the Old and the New worlds, and the consequent variations in their making and modes of incorporating citizens.

Generally speaking, the difference between the socialist and capitalist countries is striking with regard to citizenship rights in that civil and political rights were almost completely absent in the former. The fact that the socialist state abolished individual ownership of property, seizing it all for itself, rendered civil rights largely irrelevant. Similarly, the moment for political rights disappeared because of the one party system and the installation of the *nomenklatura,* which totally dominated the system. On the other hand, while substantial weight was given to the welfare component of social rights, the right of small nations to their social heritage was effectively blocked by Great Nation chauvinism in the multi-national socialist states. Which is to say that for the individuals of relatively homogeneous socialist states the possibility of maintaining the social heritage was substantial. This was also true of individuals who belonged to the dominant nations of multi-national states. The relevant point is that the differences within the socialist states were also substantial with regard to certain social rights.

The Indian situation is both similar and different as compared with UK and USA. India like them is democratic and culturally plural although her democracy is not yet firmly institutionalized and her cultural diversity is deeper historically and greater quantitatively. As for institutionalization of citizenship values, India is far behind. Her record of civil and political rights is inadequate although much better as compared with most other developing countries. The commitment to social rights was firm in the beginning but could not be implemented due to lack of material resources. Latterly, in the wake of economic liberalization, the commitment itself got diluted leading to tensions between state, civil society and market. But, the tension between political rights on the one hand and civil and social rights on the other was a democratic deficit in India, thanks to our hierarchical social structure and traditional social values. Dr. B.R. Ambedkar aptly captured it when he said: "On 26th January 1950 we entered a life of contradictions. In politics we will have equality and in social and economic life we will have inequality" (1994: 1216).

I need to comment on the notion of Indian secularism before we proceed any further because there is widespread belief in India that democracy and secularism are ideological twins. But this is far from true. The 1950 Constitution mentions the word 'secular' only once in Article 25 (2a) and that too casually while referring to 'economic, financial, political or other secular activity'. In fact, the word 'secular' was grafted on to the Constitution as a central idea through the 42nd Amendment in 1976 at the time of emergency. Although the notion got entry into the Constitution as a child of authoritarianism, Mrs. Indira Gandhi defended it by arguing that it is a tool "to reassure the health of our democracy". This paradox persists and secularism came to be stigmatized as 'pseudo-secularism'.

There are two senses in which the term 'secular' is invoked in India. First, the state according equal respect for all religions *(sarv dharm sambhav)* and second, the state keeping equal distance from all religions *(dharm nirapekshita).* The idea of giving equal respect to all religions is a *sentiment* that can be nurtured in civil society, through the media and through citizenship education. But, the state cannot foster it through fiat or legislation. This I consider has been a fundamental error in conceptualizing the notion of secular in India. The second Indian interpretation of secular is that the state should keep equal distance from all religions. This was a *structural* possibility but the praxiological aberration by the Indian state in this context is loud and clear. The state keeping equal distance from all religions can take two structural forms: (1) agreeing on a division of labour between the state and religious organizations which means the state pursuing a policy of non-intervention in the affairs of religious communities; or (2) equal intervention by the state in the affairs of *all* religious communities. But, as is well-known, while the Indian State had consciously and decisively intervened as a reformer in the case of religions of Indic origin, it played a non-interventionist role in the case of non-Indic religions.

The rationale advanced for justifying this duplicity is that the followers of the non-Indic religions, which are also minority religions, are not yet ready for reforms. This is an unsustainable argument because the resistance to Hindu Code Bill from Hindu conservative elements was substantial. The fact is that all religious communities have their share of conservatives and they tend to resist reforms. Conversely, there are progressive elements in all religious communities. The question is on whose side is the state, if it opts for an interventionist role? The point to be noted for the moment is that the idea of secular in India suffered both because of conceptual confusion created by Indian intelligentsia and the lag in implementation by the Indian State. And, the consequence has been lethal. If one chants scriptures associated with one of the religions, it is instantly labelled as communalism. (Recall the hue and cry regarding Saraswati Vandana!). But, if one chants scriptures drawn from different religions (and this is what Mohandas Karamchand Gandhi did all the time), it is designated as secularism. To wit, *sarva dharma sambhava* in effect became multiple communalism. The Indian experience has shown that theosophical and abstract moralistic principles cannot become a realistic basis for crafting a secular state. To conclude, if we want to couple democracy with secularism, the latter notion need to be recasted.

III

The contradictions that Ambedkar referred to provide the clue to unfold the sources of conflicts in all democratic polities characterized by deep economic disparity, cultural diversity and social exclusion. There are six sources of conflicts in Indian society—patriarchy, inequality, sectorality, peripherality, externality and hierarchy—all of which adversely impinge on her democratic ethos. The first three are found in all societies, the fourth and fifth are prevalent in most of the culturally diverse societies and the sixth is unique to India. The first three sources, if not attended to cautiously, will exacerbate discrimination. Patriarchy, inequality and sectorality foment conflict, even in homogeneous democratic societies. Peripherality is a source of conflict in heterogeneous, that is, multi-national and multi-cultural democratic polities. Externality is peculiar to plural and hierarchy to hierarchical societies as sources of conflicts.

Patriarchy is a ubiquitous source of conflict in all societies but its manifestation in the political context unfolds in India in the grossly inadequate representation of women, particularly in the higher echelons of legislature. The structure of legislature in India is conceived as a five-layer system—Gram Panchayat, Panchayat Samiti, Zilla Parishad, State Legislature and the Union Parliament. Thanks to the 73rd Amendment to the Constitution in 1993 that women are represented at the lower three levels to the tune of 30 to 40 per cent by 1998-99. However, they are scantily represented in State Assemblies and in the Union Parliament. The average representation of women in State Assemblies from 1952 to 1997 works out to be a measly 4 per cent (Haider, 1998: 12). Although the situation is slightly better in the Parliament also it remains dismal. In the case of Lok Sabha the average representation of women between 1952 and 1999 was 6 per cent (Seth, 2001: 81) and in Rajya Sabha it was 9 per cent between 1952 and 1998 (Manushi, 2002: 5). And, all attempts to reserve one-third seats in the Parliament for women has been aborted by political parties so far, their promises apart. This exclusion of women from the legislative bodies at the higher levels is a persisting source of conflict in India's democratic polity.

Class inequality, like patriarchy, is also a source of conflict in all societies but in democratic societies the possibility of mobilizing the deprived is greater given the freedom of association and speech and the existence of an independent media thereby accelerating the conflict potential. In India, around 30 per cent of the people are estimated to be below the poverty line and some 10 per cent are filthy rich. The remaining 60 per cent are equally divided between the new prosperous middle class and the somewhat stagnant lower middle class. The rural-urban divide further complicates the situation. According to the 2001 census 29 per cent of the population live in urban settlements and the remaining 71 per cent in rural areas. This brings in the distinction between those who can afford the 'good things of life', the upper and middle class (40%), and the majority (60%), who cannot afford what they aspire to have. But all those who can afford may not have accessibility to these things, for example, the middle and upper middle class living in rural areas. Thus, only when affordability co-exists with accessibility, one can meet his/her aspirations. Failure to meet one's aspirations leads to frustration which in turn fosters aggression leading to conflict. The constant exposure to the media, particularly the electronic media, whets the material aspirations of the people thereby further complicating the conflict potential.

When India started her career as an independent polity, she opted for the 'third way', i.e., combining planned economic development of socialist countries with multi-party democracy of capitalist countries. The motto combined economic development with distributive justice. And yet it cannot be said that the huge material disparity between the rich and the poor has gradually narrowed. Available evidence suggests that disparity has increased. Further, according to the Economic Survey of 1994-95, the rate of return from the public sector enterprises was only 3 per cent. Nor did the restrictions put on the private companies produce the intended results as licensing favoured the big business houses. On the other hand, in spite of the emphasis on distributive justice, not only did the disparity between the rich and the poor increase, but also the absolute proportion of the population below the poverty line increased. These developments prompted the liberalization of the economy, thereby conceding autonomy to the market.

While the market in India got autonomy only four decades after she became a republic, people's participation in the development process was enlisted right from the beginning, thereby laying the foundation for the formation of civil society. This is evident from the Five-Year Plan documents. However, it cannot be said that an autonomous and vigorous civil society existed in India till mid-1970s. Such a civil society emerged as a response to internal emergency declared in 1975. Birth of associations such as Citizens for Democracy (CFD), People's Union for Civil Liberties (PUCL), People's Union for Democratic Rights (PUDR) etc., mark the beginning of the emergence of civil society as a countervailing power to the state (Oommen, 1996: 191-202). Gradually, the autonomization of state, civil society and market became loud and clear resulting in numerous tensions. This is the context in which I refer to sectorality as a source of conflict in India.

Liberalization of the economy led to the gradual retreat of the state from the economic sector; the leviathan of state and the behemoth of market are in confrontation competing for their specific interests. Similarly, a large number of civil society organizations started asserting their autonomy even when they receive state patronage. Further, some of these associations even challenge the constitutional principles such as religious freedom and secularism unleashing severe strains on the polity. The point to be noted here is that while a democratic polity should accept the principle of structural differentiation and the consequent autonomization that follows, it should not degenerate into autarchy. I am afraid the expected balance is not always maintained the civil society becoming rapacious and the state refusing to rein it; the latest case being the carnage in Gujarat. Similarly, if globalization is allowed to augment the disparity between the rich and the poor and/or devastate the cultural roots of communities, it is a sure invitation to conflicts.

Let me now turn to peripherality as a source of conflict, which is a function of heterogeneity that exists in a society. Pheripherality has two dimensions, viz., spatial and cultural. In other words, in a culturally heterogeneous society, a group/community may be relegated to the periphery either because of its spatial or cultural location. When these aspects are combined, those at the periphery become the worst sufferers leading to internal colonialism. Hechter (1975), in the case of Britain, formulated the notion of internal colonialism. In its bare essentials Hechter's theoretical claim was that the survival of nationalism depended on a stratification system that informs cultural distinctions with political salience. Modern industrialization creates and accentuates inequalities between the peripheral nations on the one hand and the core nation on the other. In this process, the core nation achieves dominance over the peripheral ones turning the latter into colonies of the former. In the case of Britain, England is the core whereas Scotland, Wales and Ireland are the peripheral nations.

The situation in India is much more complicating in that there are several core nations although the numerically superior Hindi-speech community is widely perceived as the hegemon. However, most of the core nations in the Indian Union did not seek their own sovereign states; indeed that are state-renouncing nations (Oommen, 1997: 35), save Tamilnadu. But, the linguistic reorganization of India creating politico-administrative units in mid-1950s effectively met the aspiration for cultural identity of most of the core nations. But, the peripheral nations continued their struggle and 15 new states and two administrative units with regional autonomy have been formed between 1960 and 2001 (see Oommen, 2001: 21-30). And yet, the task of establishing administrative units taking into account the cultural boundaries of communities is not yet complete. While the task is more or less achieved in the case of the tribal enclave in North-East India, consisting of 12 per cent of India's tribal population, the situations in Western India with 28 per cent and that in Central India with 55 per cent of tribal population is far from satisfactory. To add insult to injury, some of the most populous tribal communities are vivisected and assigned to core nations. For example, the Bhils are divided between Gujarat, Maharashtra, Rajasthan and Madhya Pradesh and the Santals between Bihar, Orissa and West Bengal. With the deepening of the democratic impulse, increase in the proportion of middle class and the aspiration to discover and establish cultural autonomy irrendist movements with conflict potential are bound to emerge among the tribal communities of Western and Central India.

There is yet another culturally marginalized category in India, which emerged through the process of spatial dislocation and/or erosion. An example of the spatially dislocated peripheral community is the Sindhis, largely a product of partition migration. On the other hand, thanks to large-scale migration of Urdu-speaking Muslims to Pakistan at the time of partition. The Urdu-speech community, although the sixth major linguistic community in India with 43 million speakers, according to the 1991 census, is a perennial linguistic minority in India. Without an exclusive homeland and given the presumed linkage, although untenable, between Urdu and Islam, the conflict potential in this context is substantial.

Externality, the fifth source of conflict in democratic polities, is peculiar to plural societies. While democratic states by definition entitle all citizens to equality, the tendency to treat a section of the population as outsiders may also persist in civil society. In so far as a section of citizens is not acknowledged as insiders to the polity, they are being treated as an equal is an untenable proposition. In most multi-cultural societies, those who are treated as cultural outsiders are immigrants. But, in the Indian context, the situation is much more complicated because it is invariably the cultural or legal insiders who are treated as outsiders. This calls for some elaboration.

There is a basic wedge between the majority religious community and minority religious communities in India, in spite of the wide currency of ideas like 'unity in diversity' and 'composite culture'. While the tiny immigrant religious communities such as Jews, Baha'is and Zoroastrians harmoniously co-exist with the Hindu majority, the numerically substantial minority communities of India—Muslims, Christians and Sikhs—have a tense relationship with it and this for different reasons.

Although Indian Muslims and Christians are predominantly converts from native castes and tribes as their religions are 'alien' to Indian soil, they are defined and perceived as cultural outsiders to India by the 'Hindu nationalists'. This perceived externality is rendered further distant because of their presumed mode of incorporation into India—conquest in the case of Islam and colonialism in the case of Christianity. The presence of two Muslim-majority states in India's neighbourhood—one explicitly hostile and the other not friendly anymore—and the contentious issue of Kashmir render Hindu-Muslim relations particularly vexatious. In the case of Christians the source of conflict is mainly their attributed propensity to entice the innocent tribes and lower castes into their fold, that is, conversion, employing fraudulent means. The case of Sikhs is somewhat different in that their internality to India has not been questioned. In fact, the Hindu-Sikh amity has been proverbial till such time some Sikhs launched the political project of establishing an independent sovereign state. The proclivity of the Sikhs to interrogate Hindu hegemony led to their being externalized by the Hindus, although attempts are being made latterly by nationalist Hindus to incorporate Sikhs into the Hindu fold.

There is yet another process of externalization prevalent in India on the basis of language and tribe. While the principle of single citizenship, makes all Indians legal insider in all parts of the country, the reorganization of Indian states, based on language and/or tribe, renders some immigrants cultural outsiders in some parts of India. The domiciliary prescriptions by provincial states for certain entitlements and mobilization anchored to 'sons of soil' ideology by the civil society feed on each other reinforcing the tendency to define a section of co-citizens as cultural outsiders. The acceleration of the processes of industrialization and urbanization is bound to increase inter-regional migration in India. Thus, the value of equality prescribed by democratic citizenship, the demands of internal migration propelled by economic development and the propensity of identity assertions fuelled by cultural heterogeneity pull in different directions unleashing conflicts.

Hierarchy, as a source of conflict, is peculiar to Indian society in that it is located in India's caste system which not only institutionalized but also sanctified inequality through the Hindu doctrine of creation. Generally speaking, religious doctrines prescribe that co-religionists are equal in God. But this does not mean that they are treated as equals, that is, praxiological inequality exists within all religious communities. In contrast, inequality which exists within Hinduism is anchored to the theory of *karma* and reincarnation and therefore it is expected of all *varna* categories to adhere to their respective *dharma*. This is the reason why inequality engendered by the class and caste systems need to be treated as qualitatively different. The value of hierarchy is utterly antithetical to the principles of democracy and the Republic of India through the values enshrined in her Constitution has substantially unsettled it. It cannot also be denied that the traditionally disadvantaged and stigmatized caste groups also have experienced substantial social mobility in the last half-a-century. And yet it is true that the traditional value of hierarchy exerts a tremendous influence even today moulding everyday behaviour in social, cultural and political contexts. Admittedly, co-existence of the traditional value of hierarchy and modern value of democracy is a source of conflict specific to India.

IV

The burden of my argument may be briefly summarized as follows. Conflict is a ubiquitous phenomenon in human society. In democratic polities the possibility of conflicts emerging is greater in that the freedom to interrogate values and behaviour of the elite by the masses exist. But, the quantity and quality of conflicts in a society are also determined by its nature. The three main sources of conflict in democratic-homogeneous societies are patriarchy, inequality and sectorality. In the case of heterogeneous societies there is an additional source of conflict, which I have designated as peripherality. Plural societies divide its inhabitants into insiders and outsiders giving birth to yet another source of conflict, which may be designated as externality. Finally, hierarchy as a source of conflict exists in those societies wherein inequality is institutionalized and sanctified.

Indian society is a four-in-one society; it is at once stratified, heterogeneous, plural and hierarchical. Admittedly, all the six sources of conflict are present in Indian society. The fact that democracy is introduced into such a complex society means that conflicts may increase exponentially. The road to moderate conflict as it cannot be completely eliminated is to emphasize the values of citizenship. The critical minimum conditions to institutionalize citizenship in India are to promote vigorously social equality and cultural identity.

References

Ambedkar, B.R. 1994. *Dr. Babasaheb Ambedkar's Writings and Speeches* (Vol. 13), Bombay: Education Department Government of Maharashtra.

Bryce, J. 1910. *The American Commonwealth* (2 vols.), New York: Macmillan and Co.

Conover, P.J., Crewe, I. and Searing D. 1990. *Conceptions of Citizenship among British and American Publics: An Exploratory Analysis*, Colchester, E: University of Essex, Department of Government, 1-33 (manuscript).

Dahl, R.A. 1961. *Who Governs?* New Haven: Yale University Press.

Despres, L.A. 1967. *Cultural Pluralism and Nationalist Politics in British Guiana*, Chicago: Rand McNally and Co.

Fraser, N. and Gorden, L. 1994. "Civil Citizenship against Social Citizenship? On the Ideology of Contract Venus Charity" in Bart Van Steenbergen (ed.), *The Condition of Citizenship*, London: Sage Publications.

Furnivall, J.S. 1939. *Netherlands India: A Study in Plural Economy*, London: Cambridge University Press.

—. 1948. *Colonial Policy and Practice: A Comparative Study of Burma and Netherlands, India*, Cambridge: Cambridge University Press.

Giddens, A. 1985. *The Nation-State and Violence*. Cambridge: Polity Press.

Haider, S. 1998. *Women and Political Empowerment*, New Delhi: Institute of Social Sciences.

Hechter, M. 1975. *Internal Colonialism: The Celtic Fringe in British National Development 1536-1966*, London: Routledge and Kegan Paul.

Hsu, F.K.L. 1963. *Clan, Caste, Club*, Princeton: D. Van Norstand and Co.

Klugel, J.R. and Smith, E.R. 1986. *Belief About Inequality: America's View of What is and What Ought to Be*, New York: Aldine de Gruyter.

Macpherson, C.B. 1974. *The Political Theory of Possessive Individualism: Hobbes to Locke*, New York: Oxford University Press.

Manushi. 2002. No. 116, New Delhi.

Marshall, T.H. 1965. *Class, Citizenship and Social Development*, New York: Anchor Books.

Myrdal, G. 1944. *An American Dilemma: The Negro Problem and Modern Democracy*, New York: Harper and Row.

Oommen, T.K. 1990. *State and Society in India: Studies in Nation Building*, New Delhi: Sage Publications.

—. 1996. "State, Civil Society and Market in India: The Context of Mobilization", *Mobilization: An International Journal*, Vol. I (2): 191-202.

—. 1997. *Citizenship, Nationality and Ethnicity: Reconciling Competing Identities*, Cambridge: Polity Press.

—. 2001. "Linking Development, Governance and Culture: Completing the Unfinished Task of Reorganizing Indian State", in *Development and Governance: The Fresh Imperatives for Reorganizing Indian States*, New Delhi: Initiative for Research, Analysis, Development and Action.

—. 2002. *Pluralism, Equality and Identity: Comparative Studies*, New Delhi: Oxford University Press.

Rogers, D. 1964. "Monolithic and Pluralistic Community Power Structure", in R.C. Simpson and I.H. Simpson (eds.), *Social Organization and Behaviour*, New York: Wiley.

Seth, M. 2001. *Women and Development*, New Delhi: Sage Publications.

Simpson, R.L. and I.H. Simpson (eds.). 1964. *Social Organisation and Behaviour*, New York: Wiley.

Smith, M.G. 1965. *The Plural Society in British West Indies*, Berkeley and Los Angeles: University of California Press.

Tocqueville, A. de. 1956. *Democracy in America* (2 vols.), New York: Knopf.

Van den Berge, P.L. 1971. "Pluralism and Polity: A Theoretical Explanation", in L. Kuper and M.G. Smith (eds.), *Pluralism in Africa*, Berkeley and Los Angeles, University of California Press.

—. 1983. "Australia, Canada and the United States: Ethnic Melting Pots or Plural Societies", *ANZJS*, 19 (2): 238-52.

Wilson, W.J. 1994. "Citizenship and the inner-city ghetto poor", in Bart Van Steenbergen (ed.), *op. cit.*

2

Secularism, Cultural Diversity and Democracy

ROWENA ROBINSON

Democracy and the Right to Dissent

I will not begin this paper with worn-out paragraphs tracing the history of the concept of secularism in India or complaining about its 'foreign' origins. The paper takes it for granted that secularism like democracy in the sense enshrined in the Indian Constitution is one of the concepts that we have received partly through our interaction with Western discourses. In stating this, I also acknowledge, without fully agreeing with, Chris Bayly's recent argument that pre-British Indian states had developed particular ideas about patriotism and governance (Bayly, 1998).

While not quarrelling with the position that most Indian ideas about the nation derived from Western thought, Bayly puts forward the view that ideologies of good governance and forms of a kind of 'proto-nationalism' that he prefers to refer to as 'old patriotism' predated the modern period of the Indian nationalist struggle. According to him, "concepts of just rule and equity" existed which transcended the boundaries of religio-ethnic communities and came to be embodied in the "institutions of consensus making and routines of political critique" (ibid: 104-5). This was the "old patriotism of the homelands, a tradition which generally embraced locally resident communities" of all religions, even if it did not assimilate them (ibid: 105).

I will not enter into any detailed discussion of indigenous 'nationalisms' but, without necessarily dismissing Bayly's argument, I will state that even at their best such regional and local empires were almost always constructed unambiguously upon exclusions of various kinds. If religious groups or castes *were* part of an all-embracing entity, it was only in a hierarchical arrangement. The idea of democracy was certainly not enshrined except in the strictly limited sense of a ruler having to take cognizance of his 'subjects', even the lowliest ones, and their problems. Apart from the unquestioned right to rule, given the caste organization of society and polity, certain groups were inevitably in a particularly marginal position.

In other words, indigenous 'nationalisms' were not the basis for the founding of Indian nationalism, which was predicated upon the twin principles of secularism and democracy. It may be considered an irony that Hindu nationalists of today firmly grasp one end of the handle of Western political discourses—nationalism—but are more than willing to dispense with secularism. On the other hand, this may not be so much of an irony. Perhaps, they are thinking of nationalism as formulated within pre-colonial Indian empires and this was certainly not fully akin to the modern idea. It usually ends up making place for caste distinctions, the marginality of women and the privileging of Brahminical culture that are all parts of the Hindutva version of nationalism.

The argument is often made that Hindu nationalism is fundamentally non-democratic. It is possible to sustain that argument. However, it is probably closer to contemporary reality to argue that Hindu nationalists function with a particular, if not limited and distorted, understanding of democracy.

Now, it seems possible to argue that analytically democracy has two referents which I roughly demarcate here as the legal and the political. Legal democracy enshrines the equality of all citizens before law and the principle of one person, one voice in democratic politics. Political democracy usually functions in a different way, which is based on the rule of the majority. The one aspect refers to governance, the other to politics. As such, political democracy is based on the idea that rules and policies can change with the ideologies and interests of the ruling group.

The overall principle of modern democracy is, however, based on an attempt to make a match between the two ideas of legal and political democracy. In other words, the principle is based on the argument that governments and their institutions must listen to dissent, must make place for the voices of those people and groups which do not agree with them or did not vote for them. They must ensure the protection of all citizens and their rights and must render them justice. They must ensure that alternative views are sought, that these are allowed expression and that the rule of law applies in the same way to all. This is regardless of which group is in power at a particular point of time or who won the elections.

This is why the French Declaration of the Rights of Man and Citizen declares that:

> The guarantee of the rights of man and citizen necessitates a public force; such a force, therefore, is instituted for the advantage of all and not for the particular benefit of those to whom it is entrusted (Reilly, 1992: 110).

Togadia very recently expressed the view, in the media, of the BJP government and its Hindu Right allies when he argued in favour of 'electoral democracy'. This appears to be the idea that "if the majority rules, the majority has the right to make rules in its own interest". This is an idea of democracy that Max Weber had long ago sought to understand and critique. Weber has argued that (as summarized by Freund, 1968: 222):

> The relationship of command and obedience means that any domination will be exercised by a small number—a minority which in one way or another imposes its views on the majority. There is no government of all by all, nor even of the minority by the majority. The democratic system may make it appear that this is not so, thanks to the elective process and other forms of majority consultations, but in fact it is always a minority which decides and which orients the general political activity of the group according to its views.

Togadia is clearly functioning with an idea of democracy that sees it as the rule of the 'minority by the majority' and views that as right and proper. However, Weber's understanding of democracy is both narrower and broader. While asserting the power principle in a democracy—that it will always be rule by a minority—he nevertheless also indicates the critical dimension of the legitimacy of rule.

We cannot ignore the legitimacy factor in democracy or in any other system of rule: electoral democracy is supported and legitimized by law and that, in turn, by civil society and civil norms. In saying this, I am, of course, extending Weber's argument by relying on ideas from Rawls (1999) and, more critically, from Habermas (see Deflem, 1996; Habermas, 1997). While for Weber, the state draws its legitimacy from the system of legal rules which bind the polity and have a 'rational' character, for Habermas the constitutional state draws its legitimacy, in the final analysis, from the "democratic form of the political will-formation of citizens" (ibid: 73). Thus:

> Modern law can stabilize behavior expectations in a complex society with structurally differentiated lifeworlds and functionally independent subsystems only if law, as regent for a 'societal community' that has transformed itself into civil society, can maintain the inherited claim to solidarity in the abstract form of a believable claim to legitimacy. Modern legal systems redeem this promise through the universalization and specification of citizenship (ibid: 76).

Democracy is based, firstly, on the principle that all have an equal right to speak and to be heard and to expect justice (defined again on certain accepted principles) within the system. In other words, regardless of who rules or is in power at any point in time, the rights of all citizens are its responsibility in a non-partisan way. It is this principle of democracy that is linked in a relationship of elective affinity, if not of *necessary* affinity, with the principle of secularism. And, it is this principle of democracy that best protects the interests of individuals and groups in a culturally diverse nation. The reason for making this argument is that such an understanding of democracy is based on the idea of reasonableness and rational debate and discussion. These are viewed as the modes of resolution of conflicts and disagreement. It is worth quoting again from Habermas, at some length, in his description of a 'proceduralist understanding of democracy':

> The point of such an understanding is this: the democratic procedure is institutionalized in discourses and bargaining processes by employing forms of communication that promise that all outcomes reached in conformity with the procedure are reasonable. No one has worked this out more energetically than John Dewey: "Majority rule, just as majority rule, is as foolish as its critics charge it with being. But it never is *merely* majority rule... 'The means by which a majority comes to be a majority is the more important

> thing': antecedent debates, modification of views to meet the opinions of minorities...The essential need, in other words, is the improvement of the methods and conditions of debate, discussion and persuasion"...Deliberative politics acquires its legitimating force from the discursive structure of an opinion- and will-formation that can fulfill its socially integrative function only because citizens expect its results will have a reasonable quality. Hence, the discursive level of public debates constitutes the most important variable. It must not be hidden away in the black box of an operationalization satisfied with crude indicators (ibid: 304).

Again, it may be argued that I am going back to rehearsed positions and defending secularism on the grounds that it is a principle that has worked in Western polities and is therefore necessary and desirable, and that Nandy (1985) and Madan (1987), in particular, have already successfully demolished these positions. I do not happen to agree with the view that Madan and Nandy have successfully demolished the arguments in favour of secularism. And, I do believe implicitly that secularism is a sound principle for the basis of a modern pluralist political system. Nevertheless, I am not going back here to the standard or unquestioned arguments in defence of secularism.

Let it be said that one of the arguments made by scholars such as Madan or Nandy is that secularism is impossible in India because it is anti-religious in its orientation. It does not take religions or religious sentiments and religious differences seriously. It is therefore of severely limited value in a society like India, where religion shapes beliefs and identities to a great extent. It has been said that secularism tries to push religion to the private sphere, but in India it is precisely this forcible retreat that has led to the resurgence of religion in a more aggressive and violent form. For instance, Nandy says that secularism:

> chalks out an area in public life where religion is not admitted. One can have religion in one's private life; one can be a good Hindu or a good Muslim within one's home or at one's place of worship. But, when one enters public life, one is expected to leave one's faith behind (1990: 74).

He further argues:

> Much of the fanaticism and violence associated with religion comes today from the sense of defeat of the believers, from their feelings of impotence, and from their free-floating anger and self-hatred while facing a world which is increasingly secular and desacralized (ibid: 79).

Madan (1987; 1999), in turn, has breathtaking accusations to hurtle against secularism including that it is an impotent ideology that is incapable of countering fundamentalism. The privatization of religion that lies at the heart of the notion of secularism, according to him, is unreachable by the religions of South Asia; it is only an achievement of Western Christendom. Secularism simply fails to recognize the importance of religion in the lives of South Asians.

> From the point of view of the [South Asian] majority, 'secularism' is a vacuous word, a phantom concept, for such people do not know whether it is desirable to privatize religion, and if it is, how this may be done, unless they be Protestant Christians, but not if they are Buddhists, Hindus, Muslims, or Sikhs. For the secularist minority to stigmatize the majority as primordially oriented and to preach secularism to the latter as the law of human existence is moral arrogance and worse—I say 'worse' since in our times politics takes precedence over ethics—political folly. It is both these—moral arrogance and political folly—because it fails to recognize the immense importance of religion in the lives of the peoples of South Asia (Madan, 1999: 395).

Madan is clearly not an easy writer and it must be said that his argument against secularism proceeds on several fronts. Every issue is not analyzable here; my focus remains on the points raised by both Madan and Nandy regarding the idea that secularism restricts religion to the zone of the private and that it fails, in any case, to give enough importance to people's religious beliefs. Both Madan and Nandy use the critique against secularism to make arguments for the return to and harnessing of 'traditional' principles of tolerance in Indian society. It is not the purpose of this paper to contest that the 'traditional' and indigenous bases for accommodating differences must be drawn from. However, I will assert that no argument in defence of the indigenous must take attention away from the fact of the *newness* of the Indian political structure that was put in place after colonialism. The new political structure was based on an explicit rejection of the hierarchy and discrimination of aspects of traditional structures and ideologies. Hence, the defence of secularism, like that of democracy, must base itself not just on what it draws from within 'traditional' principles that may be akin to it, but on *new* ideas that we want our political system, in the present and the future, to reflect. This has been the thrust of this paper from the outset and I will return to the argument in conclusion.

While secularism in India may be considered an import from nineteenth century-Europe (Nandy, 1990: 71), its roots in an earlier period of European history are understood (ibid: 73; Madan, 1999: 394). The privatization of religion is generally attributed to the Enlightenment, when it is believed the idea of the separation of the sphere of religion and the sacred from the state and the rational sphere of public discourse began to attain importance. Reference to the Enlightenment necessitates our engagement with the ideas and influence of philosophers such as Locke, Kant and Rousseau.* Kant has, in general (and not just in discourses to do with secularism), been held responsible, to some extent, for this stress on reason, at the cost of spirituality.

It is worth, therefore, re-reading the Kantian understanding about Enlightenment. Such a re-reading is offered in a piece by Michel Foucault called 'What is Enlightenment'. I quote at some length from the text:

> Kant defines two essential conditions under which mankind can escape from its immaturity...The first of these conditions is that the realm of obedience and the realm of the use of reason be clearly distinguished...Humanity will reach maturity when it is no longer required to obey, but when men are told: "Obey, and you will be able to reason as much as you like" (cited in Rabinow, 1991: 36).

The term 'reason' here refers to a use of reason in which reason has no other end but itself. One reasons for the sake of reasoning. To the first distinction, Kant adds another: the distinction between private and public uses of reason. The argument is made that reason must be submissive in its private use, while being free in public use. Till this point we still appear to be in the domain of secularism as scholars have argued the Enlightenment defined it: private adherence accompanied by public discontent or disavowal.

But tarry a moment more. Foucault has more to say on the subject (ibid):

> What constitutes, for Kant, this private use of reason? In what area is it exercised? Man, Kant says, makes a private use of reason when he is 'a cog in the machine'; that is, when he

---

* The argument in this and the next few paragraphs has developed through discussions with my colleague Dr D. Parthasarathy with whom I have been working on issues concerning science, religion and democracy. We shall be writing with more detail on these issues in the future. I thank Dr Parthasarathy for bringing to my attention the paper of Foucault's that re-looks at Kant's views on the Enlightenment.

> has a role to play in society and jobs to do: to be a soldier, to have taxes to pay, to be in charge of a parish...all this makes the human being a particular segment of society; he finds himself thereby placed in a circumscribed position, where he has to apply particular rules and pursue particular ends...[R] eason must then be subjected to the particular ends in view...On the other hand, when one is reasoning only in order to use one's reason...then the use of reason must be free and public.

One may therefore pay one's taxes, while arguing about the taxation system publicly and freely. One may take responsibility for a chapel service as a pastor, while reasoning continually about religious dogmas. This is the characteristic of a mature state and mature individuals.

Here is a fantastic overturning of the conventional ideas associated with Enlightenment about privatization of belief. Kant is not locating belief in the realm of the private, if the private means the domestic or personal. The private is eminently social from his description of it. In other words, it is possible to adhere to religious beliefs and values, conduct oneself in religious pursuits and still partake of a modern democratic system. The condition for participation is not the dismissal of religion nor even the secret or private pursuit of it, but the admission and encouragement of discussion and debate *for, about or even against* any or all sets of ideas in the public sphere.

Here, it appears is the possibility of making a beginning in demarcating the space for secularism in the context of India's cultural diversity. How can we work out the principle of secularism enshrined in our national identity? Let me discuss some of the issues concerning Indian secularism before returning to try and address the question more directly. I do this by referring to Amartya Sen's extremely lucid and convincing article titled "Secularism and its discontents" (1996).

Secularism in India

Western observers, academics and others often tend to speak of India in terms of its majority religion. The idea that prevails is that India even though it professes secularism is a Hindu-majority country. An article by one David Frawley, available on the Internet during the recent controversy surrounding the issue of praying the *Saraswati Vandana* in schools, spoke of India as a "so-called secular country but Hindu majority in religion".

Such a mistake is cardinal. India is not a 'so-called secular country'. Secularism is central to India's understanding of itself and establishment of its idea of democratic citizenship legally and constitutionally. Indeed, it is part of a much more comprehensive idea of India as an integrally pluralist and culturally diverse country, made up of different religious beliefs, distinct language groups and divergent social practices.

To speak of India as a so-called secular country but Hindu majority in religion is to put it on par with Pakistan. When British India was partitioned, Pakistan chose to be an Islamic republic, whereas India chose to be secular. The distinction is tremendously important, as Sen (ibid) points out. It has legal and political implications. Pakistan's Constitution requires the Head of State to be a Muslim. The Indian Constitution imposes no such restriction and, indeed, India has had both Muslims and Sikhs (and others) in Presidential and other prominent public positions. India cannot compare itself with Pakistan or Bangladesh. If Hindus are marginalized or ill-treated in Pakistan, this cannot be an excuse to heap injustice on Indian Muslims. While the actions of the governments of those countries may be criticized, India cannot behave in parallel manner.

Another point to be underlined, as Sen (ibid: 27) argues, is that Muslims, for instance, are not marginal in India's population. Hindus may be in the majority, but India has well over a hundred million Muslims. This is a figure that is not much less than the number of Pakistani Muslims and is certainly more than Bangladesh's. Indeed, India is the third largest Muslim country in the world. Other minorities are also part of India's population in large numbers, and have very long histories. These include Christians, Parsis, Jains, Buddhists, Jews and Sikhs. We should also include atheists and agnostics. This is, of course, apart from the tremendous diversity of schools of thought, sectarian traditions and caste groups available under the Hinduism umbrella. Under such circumstances, it is not only impossible but also absurd to speak of India as a Hindu country.

The framers of India's Constitution, therefore, wanted to make sure that the state would not take a biased position in favour of any particular community and religious conviction. In the context of the issue of prayers in schools, it must be said that religious education in state-run schools is inadmissible, therefore, if it is only education in a particular religion. Democracy ensures that one may have schools run by different religious and cultural institutions including minority-run schools, *shakhas* or *madrasas*. The freedom to choose to send one's children to such schools is available, but the state cannot openly espouse any *one* religion. The democratic polity and openness of our system permits plurality in educational ideas and institutional practices as it permits the preaching and the practice of different cultural and religious traditions. These may flourish as long as they are not inimical to the basic principles of law and order and as long as they do not threaten the right to life or dignity of other citizens.

The argument that *Saraswati Vandana* and the Upanishads, the Vedas and Sanskrit are synonymous with India, if that means that they are linked to the idea of citizenship or that respect and belief in them is so linked, is not constitutionally valid. For one, the texts of these traditions are not representative of Hinduism, but only partially of

Brahmanic ideas. Non-Sanskritic Hindu texts abound, as do texts of other philosophical traditions within Hinduism, including secular traditions such as the Charvaka school of thought. Secondly, such texts, as indeed the body of ancient texts of any tradition—Buddhism, Hinduism, Christianity or Islam—are part of a world cultural heritage. They are not exclusively Indian and may not be linked to Indian citizenship.

In this context, we have to remember that India is not a nation-state in the sense in which some European countries might be. It is not ethnically or culturally singular. Indeed, the Constitution of India does not require it to be so. The multi-ethnicity and cultural diversity of India is accepted and sought to be preserved. The rights of minorities enshrined in the Constitution of India are based precisely on this principle. The Hindutva forces wish to sabotage the plurality of India and make it, forcibly if necessary, into a country with a single ethnic and religious identity. However, the historical, regional, cultural, linguistic and religious variety of India empirically militates against this proposal.

India is a modern republic. Its constitution is not written in Sanskrit, nor does it derive its principles from ancient texts. Its validity and also the validity of India's modern, legal and political system, which protects it and functions under it, derives its legitimacy not from our ancient legal, religious or cultural texts but from quite separate principles of law and justice. Respect for religious and cultural texts may be part of ethnic, cultural, religious identity, but cannot be a basis for citizenship of the Indian State.

Cultural Diversity, Democracy and Civil Debate

In this section, I will try to summarize the argument and return it to the original questions and ideas posed. I will argue that throwing out secularism is like throwing out the baby with the bath water. While there are several problems in the ways in which secularism is understood and practised in India, the principle is worthwhile and, indeed, indispensable. What might be remembered is that secularism is not an issue that involves only Hindus and Muslims. The innumerable regional, caste, religious and cultural variations in India cannot be protected in its absence.

One of the critical problems with the practice of secularism in India has been, as Sen (ibid) pointed out, that it amounts, more often than not, to the collective intolerance of the different communities and groups. What we have not been able to institutionalize and internalize yet, in politics or in society, is secularism based on the respective capacities for tolerance of divergent communities. On the other hand, we have to contend with scholarly discourses that dismiss secularism on the grounds that it trivializes or devalues religion.

This paper has argued that Enlightenment ideas, far from dismissing religion or arguing for its relegation to the sphere of the *domestic*, accept not only its place in modern societies but also that citizens will have duties and beliefs, practices and responsibilities of a religious nature. Such duties are, in fact, accepted alongside of and in the same breath as eminently 'secular' duties of citizens, such as the payment of taxes. Diverse religious and cultural traditions may therefore flourish in a secular India, contrary to the views of those who espouse the anti-secularist manifesto. The principles of law and order and of the rights and dignity of other citizens are the basis for ensuring that particular traditions do not infringe on public order or on the rights of others.

If the practice of religions is accepted and encouraged, what is the understanding of the space of secularism that marks such a polity? As has been mentioned earlier, the secular function might be marked by an attempt to call on and enhance the collective capacity for open-mindedness of different communities. This does not mean that the activism in favour of secularism is relegated completely to the social sphere. The legal and political framework for the enactment of such a notion of secularism draws on the ideas of democracy and the right to dissent I have spoken of in detail earlier in this paper.

The functioning of secularism till now in India has been based on different ideas. In assuming the right of communities to express intolerance, the state has created the social and political conditions for the spread of narrowness. This has simultaneously undermined the *democratic* underpinnings of the state by restricting the rights of individuals and groups to peaceful dissent and to freedom of speech and expression of opinion. Any statement or action that is likely to cause wrath to any community is instantly seen as liable for a ban. The banning of Salman Rushdie's book *Satanic Verses* is an example. It is not, of course, true that the state exercises the right to ban only in favour of the minority communities. Ambedkar's *Riddles of Hinduism* was banned, and such bans have touched many issues, including a recent play re-interpreting the figure of Mahatma Gandhi.

Sen (ibid) compares the Indian situation with the debate around the issue of blasphemy in modern Britain. The United Kingdom is formally Christian in that it continues to sustain an anti-blasphemy law that protects only Christian beliefs. While it is possible for a secular Britain to go along with demands to extend the protection of the law to all religions, it is also possible for Britain to repeal the blasphemy law altogether. Secularism is maintained in either case, but in only one of the two cases is it based on the overriding principle of the democratic right of individuals and groups to express freely views that may not be shared by others.

I began by arguing that democracy obtains its legitimacy not just from the outcomes of electoral exercises, but from the legal principles of equality and justice for all citizens on which it is principally based. The grounding of the legitimacy of democratic principles lies in the discursive opinion and will-formation of equally entitled citizens of a state. Law is grounded on moral and normative ideas, which are formed by and discussed within the space of rational civil debate. The constitution of this space is inconceivable in the absence of a Kantian right to the public use of reason. In other words, secularism and democracy imply each other in all democratic polities and, even more critically, in all plural and culturally diverse democratic polities. The democratic principle allows 'majority' rule, but is undermined if all groups are denied equality before law or the space to be heard in political and civil discussion. Adherence to religious dogma or the expressions of cultural difference in other respects are concomitant with the freedom to dissent from these, disagree with them or reason with them, about them or against them in the public sphere.

Secularism in a multi-religious and multi-cultural society like ours thereby implies neither the dismissal of religion nor its relegation to the private sphere in the hope of its eventual disappearance under the onslaught of modernity. It implies the right to practice any religion or none combined with the right to dissent from or debate religious and non-religious ideas freely in the public sphere.

The shadow of Gujarat falls heavily on the concerns of this paper and is a horrific example of the illegitimate use of an 'electoral majority' to further the interests of one group at the tragic cost of another. It is the clearest indication of the outcome of the pursuit of a Hindu nationalist political agenda, which privileges a non-democratic understanding of nationalism and abandons the pursuit of secularism according to any meaning given the term. When civil society is damaged and the judicial and administrative aspects of governance made subservient to the logic of numbers, democracy suffers irrevocably. Citizens may no longer look to the state for impartiality or justice and may no longer have any voice in the public sphere.

References

Bayly, C.A., 1998. *Origins of Nationality in South Asia*. New Delhi: Oxford University Press.

Deflem, Mathieu (ed.). 1996. *Habermas, Modernity and Law*. London: Sage Publications.

Foucault, Michel. 1991. "What is Enlightenment?" in Paul Rabinow (ed.), *The Foucault Reader*, London: Penguin Books, pp. 32-50.

Freund, Julien. 1968. *The Sociology of Max Weber*. London: Allen Lane, The Penguin Press.

Habermas, Jürgen. 1997. *Between Facts and Norms: Contributions to a Discourse Theory of Law and Democracy*. Cambridge: Polity Press.

Madan, T.N. 1987. "Secularism in its place," *Journal of Asian Studies*, 46 (4).

—. 1999. "Secularism in its place" in T.N. Madan (ed.), *Religion in India*, Delhi: Oxford University Press, pp. 394-409.

Nandy, Ashis. 1985. "An anti-secularist manifesto", *Seminar*, 314.

—. 1990. "The politics of secularism and the recovery of religious tolerance" in Veena Das (ed.), *Mirrors of Violence: Communities, Riots and Survivors in South Asia*, Delhi: Oxford University Press.

Rawls, John. 1999. *The Law of Peoples*. Massachusetts: Harvard University Press, pp. 69-93.

Sen, Amartya. 1996. "Secularism and its discontents" in Kaushik Basu and Sanjay Subrahmanyam (eds.), *Unravelling the Nation: Sectarian Conflict and India's Secular Identity*, pp. 11-43. Delhi: Penguin Books, pp. 11-43.

—1992. "Two revolutionary declarations" in Kevin Reilly (ed.), *Readings in World Civilizations (Vol. 2): The Development of the Modern World*, New York: St. Martin's Press, pp. 105-11.

3

Democracy, Cultural Identity and Nationalism in Multi-National Context

S.K. NANDA

The ideal of democracy is inextricably linked with the concept of nationalism. In fact, in the context of nationalism, the democratic ideal basically stands for the notions of self-determination and self-rule. It is popularly believed that nationalism, as a principle of self-determination, is invariably associated with the concept of sovereignty. That is, nationalism, as a sentiment or as a movement, necessarily tends to achieve a sovereign state. But empirical evidences in many parts of the world, especially culturally plural and/or multi-national countries, reveal that the goal of nationalism may vary from levels of autonomy to outright political independence. In several instances it is seen that nationalistic sentiment was invoked by people to protect their distinct cultural identity within the parameters of provincial autonomy under a common sovereign state. Such instances provide strong reasons to believe that nationalism and democracy could very well be used for safeguarding identity and autonomy. This variety of nationalism, for analytical purposes, may be termed as *cultural nationalism*. In this paper, an attempt is made to bring into focus this phenomenon of cultural nationalism in the context of multi-national countries in general and India in particular.

I

A multi-national state consists of people belonging to diverse nationality groups. Such states, the world over, experience differing levels of identity which in turn create competing claims upon the loyalty of their people. Normally, in these countries, people's loyalty to the overarching state competes with the loyalty to their respective nationalities. To put it differently, people in such cases wish to cling to their civil-political identity without shedding or tampering their specific cultural identity and the notions of ancestral 'homeland'. Shils (1957) quite aptly observed that people in such states display both civil-political and cultural-primordial ties. If the framework is disturbed in any form, there would be predictable conflict because one or another nationality may feel deprived objectively or subjectively.

Incidentally, quite a large number of multi-national states are located in the Third World, i.e., Asia, Africa and Latin America. For a greater part of their history, most of these states remained under the rule of European colonial powers. European colonialism, however, could not obliterate the multi-cultural set-up of these countries. On the other hand, it provided effective grounds for the growth of nationalism in these countries.

It may be recalled here that as a political doctrine nationalism originated in modern Europe and was exported to the Third World countries during the colonial period. But, what is interesting to note is that while in Europe emergence of nationalism aimed at establishing modern sovereign states along national lines following the one-nation-one-state dictum, in the multi-cultural colonial countries nationalism was conceived differently at different contexts. At the macro level nationalism was seen as an anti-colonial political consciousness striving to liberate the country from foreign rule and establish sovereign state. But, at the micro level, it was perceived as a form of cultural consciousness seeking to protect distinct cultural communities in their traditional homelands. Needless to say, the former represents political nationalism and the latter encapsulates the cultural expression of nationalism.

It goes without saying that the concept of nation—real or imaginary—is central to all forms of nationalism. While, in some cases, national consciousness arises from a pre-existent nation, in some it may lead to construction of a distinct national identity. By and large, in typical European sense, nation meant a culture-congruent sovereign political entity. But given the dual interpretation of nationalism, in the multi-cultural colonial world, nation acquired a double connotation. At the macro level nation acquired a political form based on shared colonial experience and geo-political unity; whereas at the micro level nation assumed a cultural form based on cultural-linguistic-territorial identity. This dual notion of nation and nationalism persists in these countries even after independence. In the independent period the macro-political unit is referred to as nation in the political sense whereas the constituent micro unit is viewed as nation in the cultural sense. In other words, in the case of multi-national states, nation emerged as a political entity at the common political level and as a cultural entity at the specific cultural level. The former is based on the political variables such as sovereignty, common citizenship and common legal-administrative system. The latter is based on the socio-cultural criteria such as cultural homogeneity, shared history and distinct language; territory being common to both the understanding of nation.

As mentioned earlier, in the ex-colonial countries, nationalism emerged as a response to colonialism. But, what is often overlooked is that in these countries the colonial ruler created provincial administrative boundaries, which did not correspond to the cultural boundaries of different nationalities. This provincial arrangement not only gave rise to disjuncture between culture and territory but also eventually lead to domination of one nationality over another in a given provincial unit. The dominated nationalities responded by asserting their distinct national identity in separatist terms. The political manifestation of such assertion varied from the demand for a culture-congruent provincial unit to a separate sovereign state.

The situation exploded after independence. The arrival of freedom, introduction of self-governments and establishment of democratic institutions provided the requisite platforms for arousal of national consciousness among the hitherto subdued and neglected nationalities. Considering the enormity of the problem, some ex-colonial multi-national countries undertook provincial reorganization on primordial basis. But, the primordial basis differed from one country to another. For example, region was the basis of reorganization in Indonesia, tribe-cum-kinship in Nigeria, sect and religion in Lebanon, race in Malaysia, language and tribe in Pakistan, etc. (Gertz, 1971).

Reorganization was undertaken keeping the following goals in view: (a) establishing co-terminality between politico-administrative unit and cultural unit; (b) maintaining the unity and integrity of the state; (c) accommodating the diverse population under a common civil-political authority; (d) promoting a 'terminal' civil loyalty to the state in place of multiple primordial loyalties; and above all (e) introducing large-scale state-sponsored modernization so that all types of disaffection resulting from the ties of race, colour, language, religion, would be displaced eventually.

Unfortunately, in many ex-colonial states, neither the desired co-terminality between administrative unit and cultural identity has been fully met, nor the highly expected 'displacement syndrome' and the much hoped-for singular loyalty to the state have emerged. What is emerging, on the contrary, is a set of multiple cultural nations co-existing under common sovereign political unit thereby allowing two notions of identity, a dual level of loyalty, a dual conception of nationality and finally double interpretation of nationalism. Given this scenario, it is quite likely that those nationalities whose language and territory are not protected will surely indulge in nationalistic mobilization demanding recognition of identity and autonomy.

It is widely believed that nationality problems grip the multi-national states of the ex-colonial world; the older and well-integrated Western states remain free from this malaise. But, the fact of the matter is that even these states receive stiff resistance from their people belonging to cultural backgrounds different from the mainstream nationality. Available empirical studies indicate that in contemporary times national movements, latent or avowed, exist among the Scots, Welsh and Irish in the UK; French-Quibecois in Canada; German Swiss in Switzerland; Basques and Catalans in Spain; Burgundians and Britons in France, etc. (Satyamurthy, 1983; Nairn, 1977; Seton-Watson, 1977). In fact, both 'state-aspiring' and 'state-renouncing' nationalisms are found in the contemporary Western world (Oommen, 1997). It follows that both the old and new multinational states experience nationality problems. In such states, people, barring a few exceptions, want to survive through home rule within a common sovereign state. Commenting on multi-national states, Smith (1973) rightly observed two polar perspectives: statist and ethnicist. The statists perceive and define nationalism from the viewpoint of mainstream culture and the unity and integrity of the state. The ethnicists, being desirous of maintaining cultural distinctiveness, insist on recognizing specific cultural nation and nationalism in the multi-national set-up. The statists advocate for assimilation of cultural nationalities into the mainstream mould; but the ethnicists incessantly resist assimilation with a view to retaining multiple identities.

Moreover, for the ethnicists subordination of specific cultural identity in favour of the overarching state identity and an alien cultural mainstream would mean many things: (a) it may run the risk of loss of identity and hence autonomy; (b) it may lead to unfettered hegemony of the mainstream nation; and (c) it may amount to loss of instrumental benefits and of equal opportunity.

II

So far as India is concerned, the magnitude of nationality problems is stupendous. Being a new state and the largest multi-national country, India faced the uphill task of reconciling national integration efforts with accommodation of multiple nationalities within the framework of a single polity. The task becomes all the more difficult as free India has adopted a secular democratic political system.

It is well known that India is a veritable labyrinth of cultural pluralism/diversity. Since time immemorial India is home to numerous languages, religions, tribes, races, castes and sub-castes. Of these elements of cultural pluralism in India, language, tribe and to some extent religion happen to be most crucial because they not only serve as important markers of group identity but also provide viable bases of nationality formation. The fact that linguistic and tribal identities in India are linked to a definite territory, i.e., a concept of 'homeland' or 'Desh' further reinforces their salience. Oommen (1988: 334), for example, argues that in Indian context 'Desh' implies not merely a territory but also a people, language, style of life, pattern of culture; in fact, a nation in the European sense of the term. Deshpande (1983) observed that the concept of 'homeland' is variously expressed in Indian vocabulary as 'Desh', 'Nadu', 'Rastra', etc. In addition, several linguistic and tribal groups in India possess distinct history, culture, myths, symbols and values. All these elements go into the making of territorially rooted cultural nationalities in Indian soil and that render India with her multi-national character. Given such a complex socio-cultural reality, any attempt to disturb the natural linkage between language, culture and homeland would surely cause disaffection among the affected people. As a matter of fact, this natural linkage between territory, language and culture was disturbed for the first time in India during the colonial period.

India emerged as a single political unit under British rule. British colonialism, however, systematically divided Indian territory into 'British India' and 'Indian India'. While administrative provinces were created to rule British India directly, Indian India comprising 562 princely states was ruled by native princes under British paramountcy. This colonial policy of keeping Indian states separate from British India was perhaps designed to thwart the development of nationalism at all-India level. It did not, however, take long for nationalism to grow in India. But, unlike Europe, Indian nationalism did not emerge from industrialization or bourgeois revolution to capture state power. It resulted primarily from the inevitable political framework of colonialism and the cultural framework of multi-national situation. Obviously, Indian nationalism assumed a liberal-political content and it evolved from a sense of pan-Indian geo-political unity and an anti-colonial perception shared by people belonging to diverse cultural backgrounds. Needless to say, a nationalist elite comprising various cross-sections of the Indian middle class mainly articulated the all-India national consciousness.

As mentioned earlier, in multi-national situation, nationalism emerged both at macro and micro levels. India is no exception in this regard. Apart from the all-India level, nationalism in India was also seen at the regional-cultural level. But, unlike the pan-Indian national consciousness, the regional national consciousness emerged as a form of cultural nationalism seeking to preserve identity and protect 'homeland' vis-à-vis other nationalities in India. It is in this sense that the regional cultural nationalism differed from the pan-Indian political nationalism which aimed at India's independence. Moreover, the regional national consciousness emanated from a cultural sense of 'pre-existent nation' defined in terms of a distinct culture, shared history, specific language and common territory. It follows that the origins of cultural nationalism in India date back to the colonial times. The rise of such cultural nationalism was mainly attributed to the existence of artificial provincial units in colonial India.

Like colonial experience elsewhere, in India too, British colonialism carved out administrative provinces which did not match the physical distribution of nationalities and their socio-cultural affiliation. In some cases several nationalities were juxtaposed in one provincial unit. For example, the Bengal Presidency contained different nationalities like Bengali, Oriya, Assamese, Maithili, Bhojpuri and a host of tribal communities. Likewise, the Madras Presidency included Tamils, Telugus, Malayalees and Kannadigas, while Bombay Presidency comprised the Marathis, Gujaratis, Kannadigas, Konkani, etc. In some other instances, a particular nationality (e.g., Oriyas, Kannadigas, etc.) was apportioned to two or more provincial units.

Juxtaposition reduced the smaller nationalities into a minority position, while apportionment led to cultural fragmentation and territorial dismemberment of some nationalities. The fragmentation of culture and territory created disjuncture among language, culture and territory as noted earlier. Thus tension and conflict resulted in both the cases. In the case of juxtaposition conflict resulted from domination of one nationality over another, while in the case of apportionment tension resulted from a fear of loss of 'homeland' and hence identity.

The mainstream nationalities, whose culture and territory were not fragmented and which happened to be in majority, emerged as dominant nationalities under favourable colonial conditions. While their culture and language flourished under colonial patronage, the language and culture of the dominated and peripheral nationalities faced serious threats. Further, the deprived nationalities perceived the subordination of their cultural identity to the mainstream as the root cause of their socio-economic and political deprivation. Thus, the fear of 'culturocide' and a sense of material deprivation motivated several neglected and dismembered nationalities to assert their national identity by invoking a sense of indigenous cultural defence and also by demanding a separate province anchored to homeland. This very consciousness of protecting and preserving one's cultural identity within a culture-congruent provincial unit gave rise to several cultural nationalisms in colonial India. The rise of national consciousness among the Oriyas, Sindhis, Assamese, Telugus, Malayalees and the assertion of tribal identity by the Jharkhand tribes are some cases in point. As mentioned earlier, these cultural nationalisms were pursued simultaneously along with the anti-colonial national movement for liberation of India.

Several studies have mentioned about this dual character of nationalism in the Indian context. Desai (1966: 368), for example, noted that from the standpoint of the united national movement for political independence, the movement of the nationalities for self-determination assumed decisive significance. Chandra (1982: 1282) observed that "development in Assamese, Oriya and Gujarati literature during the 19th century suggests that regional national consciousness was beginning to emerge contemporaneously with the all-India national consciousness". Guha (1983: 1701) succinctly remarked:

> Ever since its beginning nationalism has been developing at two levels—one at all-India on the basis of pan-Indian

> cultural homogeneity and an anti-imperialism shared in common; and another regional (Bengali, Oriya, Marathi, etc.) on the basis of regional cultural homogeneity, from the very outset the two nationalisms are found intertwined and dovetailed. Traditionally an average Indian identified with both nationalisms except in some peripheral areas.

Some recent articulations on national identity in India reiterated this thesis quite unequivocally. Karna (2000: 94), for example, observes that both language and region have shaped regional national identity in India and that pan-Indianness objectively co-exists with the regional national consciousness. Aloysius (1997) argues that both political and cultural nationalisms contributed to the making of India.

Of the cultural nationalisms that flared up in colonial India, the Oriya national movement happens to be the most noteworthy for a variety of reasons. First, the Oriyas were among the few nationalities in India whose culture and territory were fragmented in colonial times. Second, Oriya language and culture faced serious threats on account of territorial dismemberment. Third, the Oriya movement was the first cultural nationalism in British India which demanded separate province. Finally, the formation of separate Orissa province was the first linguistic province in British India.

In colonial times Oriya nationality was divided between British Orissa and Princely Orissa. Further, British Orissa was apportioned to different administrative units. The southern part was placed in Madras Presidency, the coastal tract and the adjoining areas in Bengal Presidency and the western part comprising the Sambalpur region was first placed in Chhotanagpur and then under the Central Provinces (CP). Princely Orissa comprised as many as 26 smaller principalities. The territorial dismemberment of Oriya land fragmented the Oriyas culturally and turned them into insignificant cultural minorities vis-à-vis the dominant Bengalis, Telugus and Hindi speakers in Bengal, Madras and CP respectively. Because of their longer association with the British, the Bengalis in Bengal Presidency enjoyed a pre-eminent position in matters of education, employment and administration. Obviously, therefore, the officials posted to the Orissa division of Bengal Presidency turned out to be Bengali migrants who in turn occupied all important positions in administration, law, teaching and clerical services (Bailey, 1959). In the same way, in Madras and CP, the Oriyas were economically dominated by the Telugus and Hindi speakers respectively. Initially, the Oriyas reacted to their inferior socio-economic position in every province they were appended to. But, finally, when the outsiders posed serious threats to Oriya language and culture, signs of nationalistic unity began to appear among the Oriyas. The cultural threat largely came from the Bengali chauvinists who tried to suppress Oriya language by denying its independent status and by urging the government to introduce Bengali as the medium of instruction and administration in the part of Orissa placed under Bengal (Patnaik, 1968). This was followed by replacement of Oriya with Telegu in Madras. Under the British, thus, the Oriyas faced both material and cultural deprivation.

To save their language from extinction and to preserve Oriya identity in British India, the articulate Oriya leadership launched a language agitation in the form of "Save Oriya Campaign" which eventually crystallized into a well-organized national movement under the banner of Utkal Union Conference (UUC), the first Oriya national organization (Mohanty, 1982). The UUC vigourously pressed for a united Orissa. At first, the UUC leadership favoured unification of Oriya areas under a single administration. But, the perceived danger involved in maintaining cultural distinctiveness vis-à-vis any 'alien' nationality goaded them to call for constitution of separate Oriya province. The culmination of this aspiration came in 1936 when a separate Orissa province comprising six

British-administered Oriya districts was formed on linguistic basis. The province, however, did not comprise princely Orissa. This part of Oriya homeland was integrated with Orissa province following the spread of national consciousness to the princely areas. There was no apparent external threat to Oriya language and culture in Princely Orissa. Here, nationalism resulted because of extreme economic exploitation and political oppression caused by the feudal rulers. Nonetheless, there was an anticipated fear of loosing Oriya identity had these princely areas been integrated with any non-Oriya province. Subsequently, 24 Oriya princely states were merged with Orissa province in 1947-48 fcllowing the principles of linguistic unity, geographical contiguity and cultural homogeneity (Patra, 1979). The Oriya experience brings out some serious sociological implications of nationalism in multi-national context. It points out that when a nation/nationality is artificially divided and assigned to different administrative units, the national sentiment may crystallize into nationalism. This will aggravate if the administrative arrangement leads to economic exploitation and cultural stigmatization of the victim-nationals.

From the Oriya point of view both the British and the Bengalis were perceived as enemies. But, in this perception, while the British were a common enemy at the all-India level, cooperation with the rest of the Indian nationalities was called for giving birth to political nationalism. On the other hand, the Bengalis were viewed as the internal colonizers sapping the vitality of Oriya nationalism. In this context, cultural nationalism crystallized in the Oriya-speaking land. In the case of Orissa, the two nationalisms proceeded simultaneously calling for selective cooperation with British in the context of Oriya nationalism and necessary cooperation with Bengalis in the context of Indian nationalism. The Oriya example further clarified that the disjuncture between the cultural boundary of nationality and administrative boundary may lead to nationalistic mobilization by a deprived nationality. Admittedly, this mismatch persisted in India after independence and it continues to exist even today. Little wonder, then, those regional rational movements demanding provincial states continue to emerge in India.

After independence the biggest challenge before the Indian government was integration of princely states with the Union of India. Sardar Patel, with his astute statesmanship, made this task possible. But, after integration, the political map of India retained several bigger multi-lingual units such as the provinces of Bombay, Madras, Punjab, Assam and a few bigger princely states such as Hyderabad, Mysore, PEPSU (Patiala and East Punjab States Union) etc. It may be noted that the British through various constitutional measures had visualized India as a union of autonomous provinces. Independent India inherited the same political vision and hence cultural nationalism seeking provincial units proliferated in the post-independent period.

With the arrival of freedom the political climate in India has changed. The establishment of a federal polity, introduction of parliamentary democracy and the thrust on constitutionalism not only laid the foundations of a new political era but also contributed immensely to strengthening the forces of cultural pluralism. The Indian Constitution, in fact, legitimized cultural pluralism by enlisting 14 major languages in its Eighth Schedule under Articles 344 (1) and 351. Subsequently, Sindhi in 1967 and Manipuri, Konkani and Nepali in 1992 were added to the schedule thereby increasing the number of languages to 18. In the changed atmosphere, thus, people increasingly became conscious of their primordial-cultural identity.

The struggle for a separate Telugu province was the first leading example of cultural nationalism in independent India. In fact, Telugu nationalism had its origin in the colonial period. The Telugus mainly protested against the economic and political domination of the Tamils in the erstwhile composite Madras province. Finally, the Telugu national struggle culminated in the formation of Andhra Pradesh in 1953 (Rao, 1973). The formation of Andhra Pradesh, however, opened the floodgates of regional nationalist aspirations. The situation went to such an alarming height that the liberal-democratic leadership of India had to accept linguistic-cultural homogeneity as the basis of restructuring the provincial map of the Indian Union (Ambedkar, 1955). The Indian leadership accommodated people's demand primarily within the framework of Indian Constitution. The significant step in this direction was taken by setting up the States Reorganisation Commission (SRC) in 1953. The SRC, in its report of 1955, recommended the central government for 16 states and three union territories (SRC, 1955). With regard to reorganization, the SRC broadly followed four major principles: (a) preservation and strengthening the unity and integrity of India; (b) linguistic and cultural homogeneity; (c) financial, administrative and economic considerations; and (d) successful working of the national plan (ibid.). But, finally, India was reorganized into 14 states and six union territories on the basis of the States Reorganization Act of 1956.

The reorganization of 1956 was popularly referred to as linguistic reorganization. It is true that the SRC largely followed the linguistic principle for states reorganization and did not recommend for creation of any state on the basis of tribe and religion. But, on a closer look, one finds that the 1956 reorganization created only some linguistic provinces such as Kerala, Karnataka and Tamil Nadu, while some states like Orissa, Bihar, Bengal etc. preceded reorganization; and in some other instances, the princely states having linguistic affinity and geographical contiguity were merged with an erstwhile province such as Andhra. It may further be noted that the major Hindi-speaking North Indian states such as Uttar Pradesh, Madhya Pradesh, Bihar and Rajasthan were created following historical and geopolitical considerations.

Again, going by the linguistic principle, the entire Hindi-speaking region should have been constituted into either a single state or split up into many smaller states based on the distribution pattern of speech communities such as Maithili, Bhojpuri, Awadhi, Bundelkhandi etc. in the Hindi belt. Even, the administrative viability principle was not met in the case of the bigger states like Uttar Pradesh, Bihar, Madhya Pradesh etc. The retention of the two major bilingual states of Bombay and Punjab and the multilingual state of Assam further nullified the linguistic principle. Hence, the goal of ensuring co-terminality between administrative unit and linguistic group was not satisfactorily met.

Further, the 1956 reorganization was carried out on the basis of some constitutionally recognized major languages. In the multi-lingual set-up of India, as many as 1,652 languages/ mother tongues are spoken. Out of these, 1,549 is native to India (Nigam, 1971). But it does not mean that as many states should be created for as many languages spoken in the country. Nevertheless, the people with a distinct language, sizeable strength and a specific homeland stand a better chance for having a separate province.

Besides, the identification of a constitutionally recognized language with a particular state has converted many languages into either dialects or minority languages. Also, numerous tribal languages were left outside the scope of the Constitution of India even though they are spoken by a fairly good number of people. Hence, the race for inclusion of one's language in the Eighth Schedule of the Indian Constitution escalated after reorganization. In a sense, the scheme of reorganization mainly benefited the bigger and/or mainstream nationalities; the smaller and peripheral nationalities by and large continued to remain in a state of domination-deprivation within a multi-cultural administrative unit. Thus, states reorganization of 1956 has created as many problems as it solved.

As noted above, at the time of reorganization, Bombay and Punjab were kept as bilingual provinces regardless of people's demand to bifurcate them. The discontented Marathi people launched the Samyukta Maharashtra Movement in protest against the decision (Deshpande, 1983). Consequently, as popular unrest rose to soaring heights, Bombay was bifurcated in 1960 and the provinces of Maharashtra and Gujarat were created to accommodate both Marathi and Gujarati national sentiments.

It follows that the reorganization of 1956 and later the creation of Maharashtra and Gujarat in 1960 have brought into focus a crucial dimension of Indian polity, that is, legitimization of cultural nationalism and the role of language in creation of provinces. However, with passage of time, the central government has accepted some other bases of provincial reorganization such as tribe, region and to some extent religion (e.g., religious-cum-linguistic identity, religious-cum-tribal identity).

As noted earlier, tribe provides a viable basis of nationality formation in India. Tribals constitute nearly 7 per cent of India's population and as far as spatial distribution is concerned they form an overwhelming majority in some pockets. The greatest concentration of tribals is seen in central and north-eastern parts of the country. It is generally assumed that language-based cultural nationalism is absent among Indian tribes. This is so because, most of the tribal languages are not so well developed (in terms of script, standardization and literary tradition) as to cause nationality formation on linguistic basis. Not only a large number of tribes in India are too small to constitute self-sustaining units, but some of them are utterly multi-lingual too. Probably, this is the reason why the SRC did not recommend for creation of any state on the basis of tribal language. For example, the SRC rejected the Jharkhand demand on the ground that the region lacked common culture and language.

But, the fact of the matter is that in some instances in India several tribes have been able to define their nationality both in terms of their language and tribal identity. For example, the Santhalis in Central India, more often than not, define their rationality in terms of a distinct Santhali language in addition to their tribal identity. The Santhali language is not only spoken by more than 3 million people, but it also possesses its own script called 'Ol chiki' (Mohapatra, 1986). Like the Santhalis, the Mizos, Khasis, Garos etc. have defined their nationality in terms of distinct language and tribal identity. Importantly, Khasi, Garo and Mizo languages are used as medium of instructions in school in their respective regions.

But, by and large, articulation of tribal nationalism in India is based on common tribal identity, common culture and common territorial bonds (Singh, 1984). Jharkhand nationalism, for example, has developed on the basis of a common tribal identity comprising a group of disparate tribes such as Santhali, Munda, Oraon, Ho, etc. Ghosh and Sengupta (1982) observed that a nascent lingua-franca, common cultural traits and common tribal identity serve as the basis of Jharkhandi nationalism. Although, several languages such as Santhali, Mundari, Ho, Kurukh etc. are spoken in Jharkhand region, yet 'Sadri' is considered as the lingua-franca by both tribals and non-tribals inhabiting the region (Keshari, 1982). In the case of the diverse Naga tribes, nationalism is articulated not on the basis of a distinct language, but on the basis of a common Naga identity, a Naga 'homeland' and a spoken link language called Nagamese (Mishra, 1978). In Arunachal Pradesh, tribal nationalism is expressed in terms of common territory, tribal identity and of course the link language (i.e., either Hindi or Assamese). In the Chhattisgarh region cultural nationalism developed in terms of tribal identity, economic backwardness, dialectal variation and common historical experience.

In the north-east cultural nationalism among the Khasi, Garo and Jaintia tribes emerged in protest against the language policy of Assam and the imminent Assamese cultural domination. The All Party Hill Leaders' Conference opposed the introduction of Assam State Language Bill of 1960 and demanded a separate province comprising Khasi, Garo and Jaintia tribes.

In fact, demands for creating provinces based on tribal identity were made in India ever since independence. Consequently, Manipur, Meghalaya, Himachal, Mizoram, Arunachal have been formed between 1960 and 1986 to accommodate tribal national sentiments. In 2000, three more states viz., Uttaranchal, Chhatisgarh and Jharkhand were carved out by reorganizing the former states of Uttar Pradesh, Madhya Pradesh and Bihar. It is interesting to note that in formation of these three states the official Hindi language serves as the factor of unity.

Tribal nationalism in India, barring a few, tends to accept the idea of self-rule within the provisions of provincial autonomy. But, the Nagas, Mizos and some Manipur tribes have developed secessionist orientation. The Mizo National Front, under Laldenga's leadership, clamoured for an independent Mizo State. But later the trajectory of Mizo nationalism changed from secessionism to autonomy as Mizo leadership accepted the Indian Constitution and preferred to exist as a cultural nationality in India. Subsequently, Mizoram was granted statehood in 1986. But, the Nagas so far have not been able to reconcile with the Indian identity and the Indian State. The Naga national consciousness still persists with the concept of an independent Naga state.

In addition, some tribes such as the Gorkhas, Bodos, Garos, Karbis and Reangs still persist with their quest for identity and homeland. Ever since 1980s the Gorkha National Liberation Front has been struggling for a separate province for the Gorkha-Nepali nationality located in the northern hill districts of Bengal. Similarly, the militant Bodos and the Karbis are fighting with the mainstream Assamese nationality for carving out a provincial homeland for their respective tribes. The Garos demand for separation in Meghalaya and Reang separatism in Mizoram are other instances of tribal nationalism for preservation of identity.

The case of Assamese cultural nationalism needs special mention here. In Assam, nationalism emerged in the context of anti-Bengali and anti-foreigner struggle. In fact, the Assamese national consciousness was not directed at achieving any separate province; it was rather aimed at protecting Assamese nationality from the imminent danger posed by the Bengali migrants in the initial stages and the illegal foreign infiltrators in the later period. In the initial stage Assamese nationalism was more cultural in orientation, but in later days it turned more economic in orientation.

After the formation of Nagaland, Mizoram, Meghalaya and Arunachal Pradesh, the boundaries of Assam shrunk to the Assamese-dominated Brahmaputra valley and the Bengali-dominated Surma or Barak valley. Like the Oriyas, the Assamese too faced both cultural and material deprivation because of Bengali domination. Anti-Bengali agitation broke out in Assam because the Bengalis, particularly in the Barak valley, offered stiff resistance when Assamese was declared as the official language in 1960 and as medium of instruction in 1972. The Assamese perceived the Bengali resistance as a threat to Assamiya national identity and culture. In the 1980s Assamese nationalism largely centred around nativism, i.e., economic deprivation of the native Assamese by the outsiders, particularly the illegal Bengali infiltrators (Guha, 1983; Das, 1983). Interestingly, Assamese nationalism turned secessionist with the rise of United Liberation Front of Assam (ULFA). The ULFA raised the slogan "Assam for Assamese" and thinks in terms of a sovereign Assam state.

Like language, religion also plays an important role in the growth of nationalism. Some scholars, however, dismiss religion as a basis of nationality formation because there is no necessary linkage between religion and territory (Oommen, 1986). Moreover, a particular religion may comprise people belonging to diverse linguistic affiliations. Also, a particular speech community may include people professing different faiths. Even, people having both religious and linguistic unities may differ on the grounds of geography, history, culture and political ideologies.

There is no denying the fact that secularism is the hallmark of India's polity and society. Given the secular fabric, the central leadership in India does not entertain regional nationalistic aspiration based on religion. Nevertheless, instances of cultural nationalism using religious elements are available in India. For example, the Sikh-Punjabi nationalism, which led to the formation of Punjab state in 1966, very gingerly used religious symbols in defining the identity of Punjabi nationality. Pre-partition Punjab was a multi-lingual and multi-religious province. After partition, the Indian part of Punjab comprised two major linguistic groups: the Punjabis and the Hindi-speaking people. Along religious line, the Punjabis are further divided into Sikhs and Hindus. The Sikh-Punjabis largely concentrated in the north-west part of erstwhile Punjab province differentiated themselves from the Hindus and on that basis demanded a Sikh state. The Akali Dal, which spearheaded the movement, exclusively used three prominent symbols to define Sikh national identity: (a) historical symbols drawn from the glorious Sikh kingdom; (b) religious symbols, i.e., the 'five Ks' (Kesh, Kachha, Kangi, Karha and Kirpan); and (c) linguistic symbols, i.e., Gurumukhi-Punjabi language (Brass, 1974). But, as the central government did not consider the demand purely on religious basis, the Sikh leadership changed their stand and demanded a Punjabi Suba on the secular basis of Punjabi language (Nayyar, 1969). In granting Punjabi Suba, however, linguistic-cum-religious identity was acknowledged to some extent. The supporters of the Khalistan movement did not accept this limited version of Sikh homeland; they strongly clamour for a sovereign Sikh state.

Religious element was present in Tamil nationalism also. The pro-Dravidian Tamil nationalism emerged by contrasting itself with Aryan (Brahminical) brand of Hinduism and the non-Dravidian Hindi language and culture. The Tamil leaders systematically used these religious, cultural and linguistic symbols to define Tamil national boundary as against the North (Hardgrave, 1965; Barnett, 1976). The national movements of various north-east tribes such as the Nagas, Mizos, Khasis and Garos were also laced with religious overtones. These tribes define their national identity in both tribal and Christian terms. The movement for independent Kashmir is yet another notable example of religion-based nationalism. Despite the fact that state of Jammu & Kashmir comprises the Muslim dominated Kashmir valley, the Hindu majority Jammu region and the Buddhist-dominated Ladakh region, the Muslim separatists identify the whole state with the Muslims only. In recent times the trifurcation of the state has been raised in several quarters. As per this argument the state should be reorganized to form three separate provinces, namely, Jammu, Kashmir and Ladakh. But, if this scheme is implemented, the proposed new states will surely be based on the factors of language, religion and tribe. What is, however, significant to note is that the religion-based cultural nationalisms in India share one thing in common, that is, the tendency to develop secessionist goal.

The recent demand for a separate Koshal state in western Orissa brings into limelight another variety of cultural nationalism. In this case, despite the linguistic unity, nationalism crystallizes due to tensions and conflict resulting from regional developmental disparities. As previously mentioned, the state of Orissa came into being following the rise of Oriya nationalism. But, the state that emerged finally contains two distinct regional units, viz., coastal belt and western region, which experienced differential rate of socio-economic development and political mobility. These two regions also differ in terms of geographical, historical and socio-cultural features. Basically, the western region, which previously formed a part of princely Orissa, experienced relatively low level of development and continues to lag behind the coastal districts in matters of education, employment and occupation, irrigation, agricultural development, transport and communication, rate of urbanization, etc. In political sphere also, the western region lags behind the coastal belt. Given these wide-range disparities and political inequality, regional discontent and disaffection began to grow in the relatively backward western region of Orissa in spite of the overarching Oriya identity.

This regional tension in recent times not only weakened the integrative forces of Oriya nationalism but also caused to dissipate the extent of Oriya feeling among a section of people in the western region. This section now sees regional separatism in clear nationalistic terms. It emphasizes that the people of western Orissa belong to a separate Koshali nationality, which is different from the mainstream Oriya nationality. The lead role in articulating this concept of Koshali nationality is played by the Khosal Party and *Khoshal Sammilani* formed by this disgruntled section. These separatists used selective historical, linguistic and cultural symbols to define the Koshali national boundary. It is maintained that western Orissa constituted the great Koshal Kingdom in ancient and medieval times; and the people of the region speak Koshali (Sambalpuri) language which can be distinguished from the standard Oriya speech. Also, leading cultural organizations like *Sambalpur Lekhak Sangh* and *Koshal Bhasa Sahittya Parisad* made serious efforts to develop literary tradition in Koshali language. Besides, the Koshali culture, which reflects a synthesis of tribal and Aryan elements, is highlighted to differentiate the western region from the rest of Orissa. Going by this logic, the protagonists of Koshali nationalism claim that the existence of a separate Koshali nationality implies the right to self-determination in cultural and political terms within the framework of the Indian Union. Hence, they urged the central government to create a new Koshal state on the basis of the distinct Koshali language and culture (*Koshal Sammilani* memorandum, 1993). The projection of regional articulation as a national movement under the banner of Koshali nationalism seemed to have come for two reasons: (a) practical advantages involved in defining collective identity in linguistic-cultural terms; and (b) linguistic identity and homeland are the chief bases of formation of provinces in India.

The articulation of Koshali nationalism shows that within a linguistically homogeneous province developmental disparities between regions may lead to crystallization of nationalism in the less developed region. The people of a deprived region in such a situation attempt to reconstruct their identity in more objective cultural-linguistic terms. Once that happens a regional consciousness turns into a national consciousness. In India, cultural nationalism of the mainstream Hindus also operates overtly or covertly. The ideology of 'Hindutva' and the concept of *Hindu Rastra* are articulations in that regard.

The appraisal of the Indian situation thus clearly reveals that language, culture, tribe and somewhat religion have been institutionalized as the crucial bases of cultural nationalism and hence granting of statehood. Given this socio-political reality, the drive to maintain cultural boundary within a provincial unit anchored to homeland is but natural. It may be recalled that in 1956 the political map of India comprised only 14 states and six union territories. But, by the end of 2000, the number of states goes up to 28. Thus, between 1956 and 2000, the number of states has doubled and in the process as many as 14 states, apart from the seven union territories, are created within a little over five decades of independence. Again, looking at the present-day mobilizations, it seems that the restructuring of the Indian Union is far from over. The demands for creation of such states as Bodoland, Gorkhaland, Garoland, Vindhyachal, Bundelkhand, Harit Pradesh, Vidarbha, Telengana etc. and the recent demand for trifurcation of Jammu & Kashmir bear testimony to this fact.

Most of these demands continue to persist because of the following reasons: (a) existence of the dissonance between administrative unit and cultural community; (b) urge to become recognizable entity; and above all (c) the socio-economic advantages involved in retaining identity and autonomy. The analysis of Indian situation further shows that cultural nationalism may assume a variety of forms such as irrendist, autonomist, separatist and secessionist. The irrendist type aims at unifying the vivisected territories of a nationality under a provincial roof. The autonomist and separatist types also desire to protect cultural nationality in a provincial framework. But, the secessionist type seeks to obtain a sovereign state and in that case it turns into a political nationalism.

III

In this paper, it is basically argued that people in multi-national countries invariably seek to express their national identity at two levels: political/civil and cultural. The former is meant for their state/country as a whole and the latter is reserved for their respective regional national identity. Given this different contextualization of national identity, the interpretation of nationalism as a state-seeking political movement or a form of loyalty to the nation-state (as in the case of most part of Europe) do not hold good in multi-national situation such as India. In this context, nationalism also implies a consciousness for preservation of regional national identity within a denoted homeland.

As a matter of fact, three key variables, i.e., (a) the concept of national identity; (b) the potentiality for self-rule and; (c) the co-terminality between culture and polity are important in the understanding of nationalism. Significantly, the concept of national identity, which embodies a collective identity, can be expressed either in sovereign political or in specific cultural terms. The consolidation of several multi-national states substantiates this point beyond doubt. The potentiality for self-rule can also be realized in independent or autonomous terms. Similarly, co-terminality between culture and polity can be obtained in independent or autonomous terms. In other words, nationalism may be directed at a culture-congruent sovereign state or culture-congruent provincial state. Hence, two varieties of nationalism can be distinguished in multi-national context: political nationalism and cultural nationalism. While political nationalism is invariably associated with sovereignty, cultural nationalisms mostly seek to survive within the framework of autonomy inside a common sovereign polity. It follows that nationalism can be understood without sovereignty, inasmuch as cultural nation can exist without being state endowed.

In India, nationalism acquired a sovereign-political connotation at the macro-national level and a primordial-cultural form at the regional national level. Unlike Europe, in India, many distinct nationalities did not tend to acquire their own states but preferred to retain their distinct cultural identity under a sovereign federal polity. It is this natural urge to retain cultural identity which gives rise to cultural nationalism in India. Importantly, cultural nationalism in India operates mostly within the cultural framework of national identity and political framework of autonomy anchored to homeland.

In India, the subjection of people to a common sovereign democratic state has not destroyed their cultural boundaries altogether. Because, adherence to the broader Indian identity is not welcomed by the people at the cost of dismantling their own cultural identities and their motivation for self-rule. Undoubtedly, modernization left an indelible impact on the pre-modern ascriptive values and institutions in India, but the anticipated 'displacement syndrome' did not occur as was visualized. The pace of modernization does not even curtail the tempo of 'quest for identity' calling for separate politico-administrative unit. Further, instead of being completely neutralized, the cultural ties are getting revitalized and legitimized on a wider scale under the influence of modernization, secularism and democracy. For one thing, in modern times, people all over India are increasingly getting conscious of the instrumental advantages involved in making language, tribe, region, religion etc. as viable bases of collective self-definition. The burgeoning influence of globalization in all its ramifications—economic, political and cultural—fails to undermine this consciousness of the people.

In the multi-national countries, such as India, democracy is just not seen as an institution of voting or a form of government. It is more associated with the systems of power-sharing, decentralization, and of course, the right to self-determination, In fact, democracy in countries like India plays a crucial role in shaping the politics of identity and autonomy. Democracy sustains rather than weakens regional national identity. In these countries democracy, culture and power are intertwined as far as identity politics and dynamics of socio-political mobilizations for autonomy are concerned.

By and large, in India, all forms of cultural nationalism emerge in the context of equality and identity. In some cases equality is demanded on the basis of a pre-existing cultural identity; while in some other cases, a search for collective identity is made for equality. But, in either case, cultural nationalism results from sense of cultural deprivation and domination of one nationality by another. As noted earlier, cultural nationalism in India basically uses the autonomy card and hence does not pose any serious threat to the overarching civil-political nationhood of India. The civil-political Indian identity can harmoniously co-exist with multiple cultural nationalism.

Truly speaking, cultural nationalism in India is an empirical reality and it cannot be wished away at the altar of the all-India political nationalism. Hence, there is enough reason in celebrating cultural identities than stifling them.

References

Aloysius, G. 1997. *Nationalism Without a Nation in India*, New Delhi: Oxford University Press.

Ambedkar, B.R. 1955. *Thoughts on Linguistic States*, Bombay: Ramakrishna Press.

Bailey, F.G. 1959. "The Oriya Movement", *Economic Weekly*, 26, September, pp. 1331-33.

Barnett, Ross M. 1976. *The Politics of Cultural Nationalism in South India*, New Jersey: Princeton University Press.

Brass, Paul. 1974. *Language, Religion and Politics in North India*, New Delhi: Vikas.

Chandra, Sudhir. 1982. "Regional Consciousness in the 19th Century India: A Preliminary Note", *Economic and Political Weekly*, 7th August, pp. 1282-85.

Das, Amiya. 1983. *Assam's Agony: A Socio-Economic and Political Analysis*, New Delhi: Lancer.

Desai, A.R. 1966. *Social Background of Indian Nationalism*, Bombay: Popular Prakashan.

Deshpande, Madhav N. 1983. "Nation and Region: A Socio-Linguistic Perspective on Maharashtra" in Milton Israel (ed.), *National Unity: The South Asian Experience*, New Delhi: Promilla.

Gertz, Clifford. 1971. "The Integrative Revolution: Primordial Sentiments and Civil Politics" in Clifford Gertz (ed.), *Old Societies and New States*, New Delhi: Amerind.

Ghosh, Anjan and Sengupta, N. 1982. "The Nationality Question in India" in N. Sengupta (ed.), *Fourth World Dynamics: Jharkhand*, Delhi: Authors Guild, pp. 240-54.

Government of India. 1955. *Report of the States Reorganization Commission*, New Delhi.

Guha, A. 1983. "Little Nationalism Turned Chauvinist: Assam's Anti-Foreigner Upsurge (1970-80)", *Economic and Political Weekly*, Vol. 5, pp. 1701-9.

Hardgrave, R.L. 1965. *The Dravidian Movement*, Bombay: Oxford.

Karna, M.N. 2000. "Language, Region and National Identity" in S.L. Sharma and T.K. Oommen (eds.), *Nation and National Identity in South Asia*, New Delhi: Orient Longman, pp. 75-96.

Keshari, B.P. 1982. "Problems and Prospects of Jharkhandi Languages" in N. Sengupta (ed.), *Fourth World Dynamics: Jharkhand*, Delhi: Authors Guild, pp. 137-53.

Koshal Sammilani. 1993. *Memorandum submitted to the President of India for formation of Koshal state*, Sambalpur.

Mishra, Udayan. 1978. "The Naga National Question", *Economic and Political Weekly*, April 8, pp. 621-23.

Mohanty, N. 1982. *Oriya Nationalism: Quest for United Orissa*, New Delhi: Manohar.

Mohapatra, S.K. 1986. *Modernisation and Ritual*, New Delhi, Oxford.

Nairn, Tom. 1977. *The Break-up of Britain: Crisis and Neo-Nationalism*, London: New Left Books.

Nayyar, B.R. 1969. "Sikh Separatism" in D.E. Smith (ed.), *South Asian Politics and Religion*, Princeton: Princeton University Press.

Nigam, R.C. 1971. *Language Handbook of Mother Tongues in Census*, Calcutta.

Oommen, T.K. 1986. "Social Movements and Nation-State in India", *Journal of Economic and Social Studies*, Vol. 3, No. 3, pp. 115-23.

—. 1988. "Nation, State and Ethnicity: Towards a Conceptual Clarification and an Empirical Explication", *Social Action*, Vol. 38, pp. 333-43.

—. 1997. *Citizenship, Nationality and Ethnicity: Reconciling Competing Identities*, Cambridge: Polity Press.

Patnaik, P. 1968. *Odiya Sahitya* (Oriya), Cuttack.

Patra, K.M. 1979. *Orissa State Legislature and Freedom Struggle: 1912-47*, New Delhi: ICHR.

Rao, K.V.N. 1973. *The Emergence of Andhra Pradesh*, Bombay: Popular Prakashan.

Satyamurthy, T.V.S. 1983. *Nationalism in Contemporary World*, London: Frances Pinks.

Seton-Watson, H. 1977. *Nations and States*, London: Methuen.

Shils, Edward. 1957. "Primordial, Personal, Sacred and Civil Ties", *British Journal of Sociology*, Vol. 3, pp. 130-45.

Singh, K.S. 1984. *Tribal Movements in India*, New Delhi: Manohar.

Smith, A.D. 1973. "Nationalism", *Current Sociology*, Vol. XXI, No. 3, pp. 5-185.

4

Reading Tribes in the Light of Citizenship Rights

VIRGINIUS XAXA

The broad assumption underlying the concept of tribe in India is that it is comprised of groups and communities outside the fringe of the Indian civilization. They have of course been seen as being drawn to it in the Indian history through a variety of social and political processes. Yet, the task was far from complete when India became independent in 1947. In the post-independent era, the ethos of the intelligentsia in general and the Indian State in particular in respect of tribes have been one of bringing and knitting them in the larger Indian society. This was of course intended to enable them, to put it in the phrase of *citizenship rights*, to share to full in social heritage and life of a civilized being as per the standard prevailing in the society. To this end in mind, tribes too, like any other segment of the Indian population, were conferred citizenship rights after India declared itself a sovereign democratic republic. This paper intends to examine the tribes in India in the light of the citizenship rights. Some of the questions it asks are as follows: What have citizenship rights so far meant for the tribal people?

To what extent have they been able to take advantage of such rights? Have these made any difference to their lives? Has there been any substantive contribution in tribes' share to the full in the social heritage and life of a civilized being?

Elements of Citizenship Rights

The citizenship is a status, which entitles an individual full membership of a community. It confers on individuals an array of rights and obligations. In this sense, the status of an individual as a citizen is contrary to the general notion of status, which is invariably associated with the notion of hierarchy and inequality (Beteille, 1996). The citizenship rights are the hallmark of democratic political system. These comprise of three components: civil, political and social. The civil rights are composed of rights necessary for individual freedom such as right to liberty of the person and right to freedom of speech, thought and faith. The right to own property and right to justice are other important rights in this category. Right to justice means right to be treated in terms of equality with others with regard to defence and assertion of one's own rights. Political rights include right to participate in the exercise of political power as a member of a body vested with political authority such as the parliament or their counterparts at the regional and local levels. It also means right to participate in the process whereby members exercising the political authority are elected. Social rights mean right to modicum of economic welfare and security to the right to the full in the social heritage, which means right to live a life of a civilized being according to the standard prevailing in the society (Marshall, 1977: 78-91). Heater (1999: 4) describes this tradition of the nature of citizenship as 'the Liberal Tradition' as against the other which he calls 'the Civic Republican Tradition'. The former places its emphasis on rights, the latter on duties.

Situating Citizenship Rights in Indian Context

Until the attainment of independence people in India had no citizenship status. They had no civil rights for they did not have right to personal freedom. They could not take up the occupation of their own choice nor could they be subject to the same process of law. They also did not have right to freedom of speech, expression and faith. Nor did have they political rights in the sense exercising political authority or participating in the election of those exercising the political authority. They however did enjoy a modicum of social rights in the sense of social security. This came from the social arrangement of caste. Thus security was enjoyed within the overall framework of hierarchy and inequality. This meant that social rights were derived from the status, hallmarks of which were class and hierarchy. Further, security so enjoyed was localized. Under the British, some rights were bestowed upon the people at large not so much as a part of the entitlement to rights but more so as a corollary or end product of the colonial administration. For example, the British introduced uniform civil law and administration. In the process, people, irrespective of their castes and creed, came to be governed and administered by same law unlike in traditional Indian society, which was governed by laws contingent to their caste position. Thus emerged the process of the right to justice in the Indian society. Indeed, many of the facets of the citizenship which people did come to enjoy though in a very limited sense came not as part of the drive to equality as was the case in Europe but as part of the general process of societal development under the colonial regime. The processes of industrialization, urbanization and introduction of modern education destabilized the fetters at work in the traditional Indian society and opened up the scope for social mobility. Social mobility after all posed challenge to the lack of freedom and equality inherent in birth-based status. It opened up a degree of freedom and to that extent it was a move towards equality but of a certain kind. There were some other rights too, which people came to enjoy but these were won over them through struggle during the course of freedom struggle movement. The right to freedom of speech and expression, however limited it may be, was one among them. Rights so won over were more of the civil domain than the political and social. Some political rights too were won over during the colonial period but they were again limited in nature and scope. After all, rights so granted were not opened up to people at large but were restricted only to people of social and economic standing. With creation of wealth in the form of property one could have acquired political rights during the colonial period.

The scene changed dramatically after independence. India adopted a constitution, which committed itself to extend not only civil and political rights but also social rights. The spirit underlying these rights was the ideology of social justice, liberty, equality and fraternity. In so doing it made a radical departure from a tradition, which was based on an ideology of inequality and hierarchy on the one hand and lack of freedom and social justice on the other. To use Beteille's formulation, India moved from harmonic to disharmonic system with the adoption of the Indian Constitution. That is, India committed itself to the ideology of equality but the social system it had was characterized by hierarchy and inequality, quite contrary to the past which was characterized by inegalitarianism both in terms of ideology and practice (Beteille, 1974). For millions living under hierarchy, inequality and lack of freedom, this was indeed a landmark development in the Indian history. It opened up vistas of freedom and justice for them.

What is however even more interesting is that all these rights, viz., civil, political and social rights, came at the same time in the case of India. In Europe, these rights came, rather won over, at different times. The civil rights are traced back to the eighteenth century, political rights to the nineteenth century and social rights to the twentieth century. The successive rights were built on the foundation laid by the previous rights (Marshall, 1977: 78-91). It was not so in case of India. The preamble to the Indian Constitution, for example, promises to all its citizens justice—social, economic and political, liberty of thought, expression, and faith and worship, equality of status and opportunity and to promote fraternity assuring the dignity of individual and the unity and integrity of the nation (Bakshi, 2000: 1). It is important to note that the Indian Constitution talks of the nation. It is doubtful if the political scientists and sociologists would talk of in the similar vein. At the same time, it is also important to note that the rights so enshrined in the Constitution had not emerged out of strong movements and mobilization against the iniquitous caste system. The freedom movement, at the backdrop of which the citizenship rights in the post-independent India are to be understood, did not have very strong current of mobilization against inequality and especially the caste hierarchy and principles. This is not to deny the long history of protest movements against the inequity of the caste system. These had either taken the forms of reforms initiated by the enlightened upper caste social reformers or more specifically movements and social mobilizations by those lower in the rung of the caste social hierarchy.

Citizenship Rights and Tribes

Indian society is marked by plurality. Of the pluralities, language, caste, religion, tribe are the major ones. The status of citizenship does not make distinction on these bases. The status so bestowed assumes place of crucial importance in the context of groups and communities, which have been hitherto at the margin of or outside the society in reference. What significance do they attach to development such as this and how have they made sense of it is an interesting question. Do these rights mean the same for people belonging to different castes, class and status? Do they stand of the same importance for them all? Equally important is to examine the extent they have been able to exercise the rights so conferred on them. After all, the marginalized groups are far from homogeneous ones. They are situated at different contexts with varying experiences, interests and aspirations. Hence, it is not possible to examine the issue of citizenship in the context of marginalized groups as such. The paper therefore makes an attempt to examine them in the context of tribes in India. Tribes, as we all know, have had experiences quite different from those in the caste organization and its fringe.

It may be kept in mind at the outset that the citizenship rights are individual rights, whereas tribes are groups or communities. Individuals have, at the same time, no social existence outside of their community/society. Rather, they can only be understood in and through the society. In a pluralistic society like India, individuals are invariably members of this or that community. Not only that but also individuals as citizens have the right to work for the welfare and development of their community as well as for the safeguard and protection of its identity. This is how the dominant communities in India, whether linguistic or religious, have consolidated their position in the society. All these are, of course, subject to the rights of other individuals as citizens. In reading tribes as citizens, therefore, I am treating tribes both as citizens as well as members of the tribal community.

The tribal people, unlike those in the caste organization, had no history of drive for equality. The drive they had was for autonomy and independence. This being the case, the constitutional provision securing citizenship rights to its people has been major breakthrough for the scheduled castes and other lower caste groups. Such has not been the case for the tribes. After all, as observed earlier, citizenship rights at least in the liberal tradition has stemmed primarily from the drive to equality. The tribes were not a part of the social system that was built on the principles of inequality and hierarchy. Hence, they did not have to go through the kind of experience of discrimination—social, political and cultural—that the lower caste group, especially the scheduled castes, had to go through. Correspondingly, civil and political rights, which the Constitution extended to its citizens, were not of great importance for tribes as was the case with the castes lower in the caste hierarchy. The problems of the tribes stemmed not so much from within as from outside. If at all they were constrained in their enjoyment of freedom and equality, it came more from outside in the form an alien state structure—to begin with British rule and post-independent Indian state later. That is, whereas they continued to enjoy rights existing within their own society, there was curtailment in the enjoyment of these rights after their incorporation into the larger society. Not only was there curtailment in the enjoyment of their existing rights but even as the constituents of the larger Indian society, they had little rights in it. Rather, as constituents, they came to suffer similar, if not same, disadvantages as those ranking low in the structure of the caste hierarchy. At the same time, neither did the tribes as collectivities had the aspirations and desires to be member of the larger Indian society. That explains as to why tribes' struggle has always been for greater control over their land, forest and other resources through articulation of political autonomy than share for greater participation and control of the state structure and institutions. Thus, what they aspired for was a space to determine their life in their own way, which of course also meant control over resources where they lived.

The socio-political and economic forces at work have been too strong for tribes to be able to resist the alien social forces. The net result has been their incorporation into the larger political and economic system in which they have been given the same rights and status as has been accorded to others, especially after the adoption of the Indian Constitution. It was an achievement only in so far as the larger society made them an integral part of that society and gave them same rights as those enjoyed by the other members of the larger society. However, the securing of citizen status hardly mattered to them for in the structure of their relations they already enjoyed these rights among themselves. In the traditional social settings, tribes already had the examples of equal citizenship and these included all dimensions of citizenship, viz., civil, political and social. Of course, it is doubtful if it could be conceived as the citizenship for rights so enjoyed have invariably been local. Citizenship, in contrast, is by definition national. In other words, citizenship is at work in societies based on territory than on kinship.

Tribes enjoyed those rights not so much in their capacity as a member of political community but in their capacity as member of the society. Rather, the political dimension was embedded in the general structure of the social relationship of those societies. After all, the political institutions were yet to emerge as distinct and differentiated institutions in the tribal societies. Yet rights so mentioned in the context of the traditional social settings had certain limitations, both in terms of reach and scope. Not only that but also limitations were strong on civil and political dimensions of rights than on social/economic dimension. There were limitations in terms of reach as there were sections within the society, which did not have some of the rights under the jurisdiction of citizenship. Women could be identified as one of such sections. It is a fairly established fact that although women enjoyed same rights as those by men in spheres like freedom to marry person of one's choice or divorce or free movement outside their home and work etc., there were as yet many limitations. The customary law and tradition at work in tribal societies put women at a disadvantageous position, especially with respect to property and inheritance. To couch it in terms of citizenship rights, women did enjoy the right to personal liberty, and right to freedom of speech and faith, right to justice etc. If at all there were limitations with regard to the visibility of these rights in the tribal society, it has more to do with relatively undifferentiated structure of those societies than the rights *per se*. Disadvantages suffered by women were however the most glaring in public domain. Neither did they have say in the decision-making process affecting public domain nor could they hold office and position falling in this domain. In other words, political rights are something, which women in traditional social settings were deprived of.

Besides women, there were other sections too, which did not have such rights, especially those, which were identified as commoners in some of the tribal communities. It is of interest to note that the tribal societies, though relatively egalitarian, are not altogether devoid of inequality, especially of rank and status. In many tribal societies tribes were divided into chiefs, nobility, commoners etc. Such was the case, for example, among the Lushais of Mizoram, Kukis of Manipur, Khasis/Jantias of Meghalaya, Semas and Konyaks of Nagaland, Akas and Khamptis of Arunachal Pradesh etc. (Misra, 1979). The examples are not exhaustive but illustrative. In some of the tribes there existed even slaves. Now, the position of the commoners in certain sense was similar to those of the women. There were still other problems. It may be noted that in many tribal communities, the office of the village chief/head or even the religious head was confined to members of a particular lineage/clan. In this context, even men, of course, of other clans/lineage could not have access to the offices though they may participate in the decision-making process affecting the village and community. Besides, citizenship rights conferred by the state have expanded the scope and base of rights existing in the tribal societies.

Civil Rights

It will be interesting to examine the way and the extent tribes have tried to make sense of the citizenship rights. This may be discussed with respect to each of the components of citizenship rights. Of the civil rights, that is, freedom of thought, expression, faith, occupation and right to property and justice, the most vulnerable has been one of property. A large number of tribal groups in India have been dependent mainly on agriculture for their livelihood. They enjoyed proprietary rights either individually or collectively over their land. Besides, they also had usufructuary rights over forests and other kinds of common property resources. It is in access to these that tribes enjoyed rights of social and economic security or social and economic rights. In the traditional social settings, right to property was not only an element of civil domain but also social right domain. However, the history of the last two hundred years, including the years of the post-independence era, has been marked by rampant alienation of land from tribes to non-tribes, especially in regions other than the north-east India. In the post-independence era, the alienation has been justified on the basis of right to make property and right to settlement in anywhere in the country. The right to property of one has been the right to dispossession of property by another. The paradox is that dispossession has invariably been of tribes. The enjoyment of civil rights on the part of some sections has been the root cause of the loss of both civil and social rights by another. Of course, tribes had been provided with security to this effect in terms of legislation. The legislation against alienation of land from tribes to non-tribes began during the colonial period. In the post-independence era of economic development with social justice, such legislation has been enacted in almost all states where tribal groups/communities live. Yet violation of such rights through legal and illegal means has gone on unabated. Tribes, of course, could go to court of law for restoration of justice. But, it is a long-drawn process and one requires resources and assistance, which the state did not make available. Indeed, the right to justice in terms of restoration of rights was left to the goodwill of tiny committed bureaucrats and administrators. The right to justice was thus closed to tribes in the absence of legal and social support from the state. The tribes could not enjoy civil rights as they had little social and economic rights at their disposal.

The other area where tribes have been vulnerable in terms of exercise and enjoyment of civil rights has been in the domain of freedom of faith and practice. Tribes have their own distinct religion which, in the absence of any specific name, has been described as tribal religion. Earlier, in the census, they have been described as animists. Tribes have however been drawn to other religions and have in course of time become the Hindus or the Christians or practitioners of other major religions. This process has been continued even today. However, the conversion of tribes to Christianity has come under severe attack on the ground that they invariable take place under coercion, enticement, fraud etc. Even if there has been conversion out of one's own free will, it is being camouflaged as having taken place under means referred above and tribes so converted are intimated, coerced and attacked. Indeed, in a number of states, freedom of religion bill has been passed with a view to prevent conversion among the tribes. In a sense, then, there is attack on civil rights of the tribes as citizens. Again, the question here is not of conversion alone. Rather, there are larger issues connected with citizenship involved. It is to be underlined that tribes have their own traditional religions. However, they are not being given the right to express and maintain this religious identity. Ever since the adoption of the Indian Constitution, they are either being constrained or coerced into not to declare their traditional religion but declare themselves as the Hindus. There may be similarity between traditional religious practices of the tribes and the Hinduism but that does not make them Hindus. Similarly, there may be similarity between traditional religious faith of the tribes and the Christians but that does not make them the Christians. However, the social and political activists of the 'Hindutva' forces have been building pressures, working out strategies and manipulations to ensure that tribes enumerate themselves as the Hindus and not as animists or the followers of the tribal religion in the census enumeration (Xaxa, 2000). Indeed, not so many months ago, the pamphlets had been distributed in Jharkhand with a view to wipe out Santhals. Mundas and Oraons for their refusal to enumerate and declare themselves as the Hindus.

The other important component of civil rights, which is consistently being violated in case of tribes, falls in the realm of language and culture. Article 19(5) of the Indian Constitution ensures cultural or linguistic minority the right to conserve its language and culture. This right is a part of the general right to freedom of speech, expression and faith. Yet tribes have been unable to safeguard and promote their language and culture. This means that tribes as individuals and groups have the right to use their own language, practise their own religion, study their own history, culture, tradition, heritage etc. The state cannot by law enforce upon them any other language or culture. Now, the state may not have enacted any legislation to this effect but in actual social reality it is precisely doing the same. The strategies through which this is being accomplished are two-fold: one is by opening up schools and imparting instructions through the language and culture of the dominant community; and the other is by not taking any positive steps worth the name towards meeting the provisions of the Constitution meant for the tribes. It was/is surely asking too much from the tribes to take initiative towards protection and safeguard of their language and culture at a stage of the social formations to which they were placed. They were economically, socially and educationally too low to take any concrete measure on the question. This explains as to why in the western, northern and southern India, there had been so much erosion of the tribal language and culture in comparison to eastern and northeastern India. Indeed, the promotion of language and culture has been left to the tribals to take care of them. Yet, because of lack of control over human, organizational and financial resources, the tribes have not been able to take effective measures in this direction. It is only when such support has been made available in some form or the other tribes have been able to protect and safeguard their culture and language (Xaxa, 2001).

Political Rights

The exercise of citizenship rights by tribes is the most pronounced in the domain of politics. This is evident both in respect to right to vote as also in respect to right to be elected. However, the moot question is whether tribes would have been in a position to represent themselves as citizens if there were no special provisions for them. The answer is emphatic negative. They would have surely participated as voters/electors but surely not as elected to exercise the political authority. Rather, they would have been represented by non-tribes. Thus, it is not so much the right to be elected as the provision of reservation that has been the most crucial in the context. In the absence of reservation, the citizenship right to be elected would have been meaningless. At least, this would have been the case in the early phase of the electoral politics if not today. This can be inferred from the composition of the political parties of all ideological persuasions at the time of independence. In fact, tribes had either no place or negligible place in the structure of the most of the political parties at this stage. There had been little participation of the tribes in the national political parties and hence the question of their representation in the absence of reservation would have hardly been possible. The access to the political decision-making process, which in a democratic set-up is made possible only through election, requires resources (physical and human) which tribes were not able to afford. Hence, had there been no reservation, there would have hardly been any serious and systematic effort on behalf of the political parties to recruit tribes to its cadre. The fact that most of the political parties were constrained to build cadre from within tribes arose from the constitutional compulsion of the reservation for them in the parliament and state legislatures. Even after cadre has been built from within, tribes have on the whole been deprived of position of importance in the political parties. Such situation cuts across political parties of all persuasions. This is not only the case with political parties but even with the trade unions. The tea garden labour force in West Bengal and Assam comprises primarily tribes. It is a different matter that the scheduled tribe status has not been accorded to them in Assam. Now, there are a large number of trade unions affiliated to different political parties, which have been working among the tea garden population. Yet, the leadership of the trade union has always been in the hands of people from outside the tribe and outside the labour force. It is only in the very recent years that one can see shift in the social composition of the trade union leadership in tea gardens of Assam and West Bengal. This is a clear pointer to the fact that if there were no obligations of the political reservation, tribes would have been at large represented by the non-tribals than tribals.

While the provision of such political participation helped expand scope of the tribal leadership and many gained materially as well as non-materially in the process, such benefits have been of limited nature and scope. After all, in terms of providing space towards protection and welfare of the tribes through control over land, forest and other resources, it has made little contribution. In view of exercise of political rights from time to time at different levels, there has been however heightened political awareness, interest articulation and aspiration among the tribal people. Indeed, politics and political mobilization are seen as the only option left for tribes towards protection and promotion of their interests. Hence, it is through political mobilization and political articulations that tribes are attempting to safeguard and promote their social and economic rights today.

Social Rights

It is in respect of social rights that tribes have been the most vulnerable. Tribes have been enjoying social security and protection in view of the control they had over land and other resources. The control over resources stemmed either from the ownership or usufructuary rights that they had over these. It is precisely these rights that they enjoyed in the past, which are in the process of erosion now. These have been taking place in either of the two ways. The incorporation of tribes into the colonial state structure through annexation of their territories also led to their incorporation into the larger system through means of transport and communication and penetration of capital on the one hand and land, labour and credit markets on the other. These processes drastically altered the relationship of tribes with land, forest and other resources of their livelihood. Traditionally, these resources were either individually or collectively owned. If they had no such rights, they had at least usufructuary rights over these. But, due to processes unleashed by the state during the colonial period to begin with and post-independent India at a later stage, there has been steady erosion of control and use over these resources by tribes. This has taken place in one of the following ways: The incorporation of tribes into the larger social system opened up the tribal areas to people from outside the region as never before. This led to a large-scale migration of non-tribals into tribal areas. This movement was not confined to mere movement for employment, trade and commerce. Rather, this also led to greed, fraud, coercion, manipulation etc. and tribals found themselves increasingly uprooted from their land and resources in a scale unprecedented in their history. The process of land alienation through such processes that began during the British rule had gone unabated in the post-independence period. In order to deal with the problem of alienation land from tribes to non-tribes, laws have been enacted in almost all states where there are tribal populations. In some parts such laws have been in existence since the British period such as the Chhotanagpur Tenancy Act, 1908 or the Santhal Pargana Tenancy Act, 1940. In the post-independence period, all states with tribal populations have enacted legislations not only for the prevention of alienation of land from tribes to non-tribes but also for its restoration. The protection towards land has also been ensured in certain parts through the arrangement such as the 5th and 6th schedules of the Constitution of India. Despite this tribal lands have gone on passing from tribes to non-tribes. This means that the legislations and constitutional provisions alone are not adequate for ensuring the social and economic rights of the tribal people. Rather, these need to be complemented and supplemented by the effective administrative, infrastructure and financial support. In respect of provisions for which certain support systems were made available, for example, the provision of protective discrimination, such arrangements did lead to some results, however inadequate they may have been. But, where such measures were non-existent or largely ineffective, the provisions made in the Constitution or in laws have hardly led to any desirable results in favour of tribes.

It is not only that the effective social and economic rights were not evolved and extended to tribes but even rights that they enjoyed, such as land and forest, were taken away from them by the colonial rulers first and then by the post-independent Indian state. The uprootedness had been compounded by the state action of development, especially in the post-independence era. Thus, the major source of uprootedness in the era has been the state itself. The large-scale industrialization and exploitation of the mineral resources and the construction of irrigation dams and power projects have thrown more people from their land and made them landless, jobless and homeless than the transfer of land from tribes to non-tribes. During the first three Five-Year Plans, more than 50 thousand scheduled tribe and 10 thousand scheduled caste families were uprooted from the Jharkhand area of Bihar alone to make land available for the construction of public sector projects. The total number of displaced families would be much higher if one were to take into account the private sector and coal mines that belonged to the private sector (Sengupta, 1979). The state projects of national development, whether industry, irrigation, power or exploitation of the mineral resources, may have benefited the country and contributed to general good but it is surely did not contribute to the good of the tribal people. Of course, the state has been sponsoring the projects of tribal development but the most of such projects are of little consequence if tribes lack resources to fall back upon.

Conclusion

Tribes in terms of citizenship rights hold the same status as those accorded to members of any other community. And, yet, in terms of enjoyment of these rights, the position of tribes in comparison to others has been extremely vulnerable. As citizens, they have suffered the most mainly due to the legacy of disadvantages, which had been cumulative. The disadvantages have been demographic and historical on the one hand and ethnic and structural on the other. The structural disadvantages, characterized by a combination of economic, political, social and cultural dimensions, emerge from the general feature of subordination of the tribes after their incorporation into the larger social system. The disadvantages suffered have however been far from even in respect of the different components of the citizenship rights. In retrospect, one could see some positive developments on civil and political fronts, especially on the latter. Yet, even these positive developments have not been solely due to civil and political rights *per se* but due to social rights in the form of reservation and other policy measures meant for the welfare and protection of the tribes. At the same time, provision of such social rights in themselves is meaningless if people concerned either lack the required resources or effective institutional support is not made available to them. Indeed, where such support has been made available, tribes have at least made sense of the citizenship rights enshrined in the Constitution of India. All the same even here achievements on the whole have been far from satisfactory, especially with regard to civil rights. It is however on social and economic fronts that the results have been the most inadequate. Hence, tribes today are increasingly taking recourse to civil and political rights, especially the latter, with a view to promote, protect and safeguard their social and economic rights and interests.

References

Bakshi, P.M. 2000 (Reprint). *The Constitution of India.* Universal Law Publishing Co. Pvt. Ltd., Delhi.

Beteille, Andre. 1974. *Studies in Agrarian Social Structure.* Oxford University Press, Delhi.

Beteille, Andre. 1996. "The Mismatch between Class and Status", *The British Journal of Sociology,* 47(3).

Heater, Derek. 1999. *What is Citizenship?* Polity Press, Cambridge.

Marshall, T.H. 1977. *Class, Citizenship and Social Development.* University of Chicago Press, Chicago.

Misra, B.P. 1979. "Kirata Karyokiness: Modes of Production in Tribal Societies in North-East India" in Das, A. and Nilkant, V. (eds.), *Agrarian Relations in India.* Manohar, Delhi.

Sengupta, Nirmal. "Class Structure in Jharkhand", *National Labour Institute Bulletin,* 5 (7-8).

Xaxa, Virginius. 2000. Tribes, "Conversion and Sangh Parivar", *Jnanadeepa,* 3(1).

—. 2001. "Tribes and Their Legal Entitlements in Castelino", in Herman (ed.), *Human Rights Education in Schools and Colleges.* Gujarat Sahitya Prakash, Anand.

5

Homogenization of Shared Spaces

Interrogating "Celebration of Differences"

VINOD K. JAIRATH

While the postmodernists question the rationality of modernity and the Enlightenment project of the West, there are serious doubts about their own 'celebration of diversity' because of rampant violence based on the politics of difference. If, on the other hand, democracy brought about, or claimed to have brought about, greater equality of individuals by obliterating the differences based on hierarchies, then politics of difference brought forth the voices from the 'margins' or 'subaltern classes' by assertion of their cultural diversity. However, just as the homogenizing hegemony of the modern West tried to make the voices of the 'Others' inaudible, so are the aggressive identity war cries fragmenting the possibilities of larger collective solidarities in the present postcolonial global village.

Let me clarify that here the argument is not against the voices from the margins which have raised the banner of revolt against the homogenizing tendencies and discourses. But it is against the *exclusionist* 'politics of identity', practised by some of the ethnic mobilizers, which is turning increasingly aggressive and violent. We need to interrogate the nature of this politics of identity that is reactionary internally and creates barriers against the 'Others' by homogenizing shared spaces. Therefore, I am arguing for recovery of 'shared spaces' in strengthening democracy, outside the politics of assimilation as well as isolation or separation.

As Gurpreet Mahajan asserts: "The need to accommodate social differences while simultaneously respecting the rights of equal citizenship has posed new challenges for democratic theory" (1998: v). We find that there are no easy answers to these challenges.

In democratic theory, according to Mahajan, "the notion of equality provided a norm on the basis of which certain kinds of differentiations were identified as sources of discrimination and social injustice. In other words, the principle of equality offered a basis for anchoring the claims of the excluded and discriminated peoples" (ibid: 3). Sources of discrimination that the democratic theory tried to overcome included noble birth, status, class, religion, race and gender. The equality, however, was concerned mainly with the political domain, as equal rights of citizenship. Mahajan goes on to state that "the issue of economic equality was rarely addressed in democratic theory...(and) this socialist impulse was always strongly contested in the discourse of democracy" (ibid: 4). The *intra-group* inequalities, that is, economic, and consequently political, inequalities *within* groups or communities, based on caste, religion, race, language, region and gender, were of no consequence.

Theorists of cultural difference challenge the 'abstract egalitarianism' of the liberal democratic theory. "The ideologues of the new ideal were critical of the principle of formal equality on the ground that it obliterated differences" and, therefore, these needed to be emphasized (ibid: 7). Abstract egalitarianism "camouflaged the cultural biases of the nation-state" such that, in multicultural societies, it is the dominant groups, which actually exercised their control over the 'other' marginalized communities. Among other things, "it imposes the same dress code on the white Christian and the Muslim woman. On all such occasions, by treating the dissimilar as similar, it places the 'other' (the marginalized) at a disadvantage" (ibid: 7-8). The uniform laws of the nation-state put some communities at a disadvantage because these laws are not 'entirely neutral'. Now, this celebration of difference opens up several new issues.

> The political implications of this point of view are also quite far reaching. To begin with, it problematizes the category of the nation-state. In place of a cohesive nation, it divides the political community into culturally discrete groups—the majority and the minorities. Further, it suggests that democratic governance in multi-national and multi-cultural societies requires different sets of institutional arrangements (ibid: 9).

Certain versions of celebration of difference brought about another significant change. Assertion of cultural identities, in many cases, also implied creation of barriers between different communities. "If assimilation was the unifying urge of policies that invoked the notion of formal equality or non-differentiated self, segregation was the ideal pursued in the renewed assertion of cultural differences" (ibid: 10). The policy of 'inclusion' was being challenged by acts of 'exclusion', at least in several cases, if not all.

These historical conditions are confronted by utopian images of multi-cultural societies. Recently, A.R. Momin, while reviewing a work of Bhikhu Parekh, states that "multi-culturalism entails a set of value premises such as tolerance and accommodation of diversity, peaceful coexistence in a democratic framework, respect for human rights, sensitivity towards the beliefs, feelings and cultural traditions of people different from one's own, magnanimity and compassion, and a commitment to the resolution of social and ethnic conflicts through dialogue and reconciliation" (2002: 101). One may not have any quarrel with these ideals. But, it is important to understand how this 'celebrating diversity' has been variously interpreted and with what consequences. Momin is conscious of the nature of struggles and manipulations that exist in the political system when he is cautiously critical of Bhikhu Parekh and states that Parekh's "conceptualization of human nature appears to be a little too idealistic and romanticized in that it ignores the dark side of human nature as reflected in irrationality, selfishness, viciousness, aggressiveness, jealousy and so on" (ibid: 104). In fact, Parekh himself finds the task of carrying out the project of "cherishing plural cultural identities without weakening the shared and precious identity of shared citizenship" very daunting. "This is a formidable political task and no multicultural society so far has succeeded in tackling it" (2000: 343, quoted in Momin, 2002). Criticizing the assimilationist, inclusive and homogenizing policies of nation-states, Parekh finds in such societies a tendency to become "closed, intolerant, averse to changes, claustrophobic and oppressive..." (ibid: 170, quoted in Momin, 2002). It is surprising that such tendencies are not noticed within the diverse communities, aggressively asserting their identities while excluding the 'Others'. These may be majority communities or minority communities. The growing inter-community hatred and violence in various regions throughout the world demands a rethinking of 'celebrating diversity' and its consequences.

What we need to examine is the following: Who are the stakeholders in 'identity politics' or ethnic mobilization? What are the motivations of different stakeholders? Who has the largest stakes in identity politics? We also need to examine the internal social, economic and political structures of communities. Who is in control of the communities and how is this control maintained? Whose power is threatened by democratization within the communities? Who construct the discourses of exclusion and hatred?

Reviewing the work on Hindu-Muslim conflict in India, Shail Mayaram (1997) has examined various perspectives such as the primordialist, the instrumentalist, the colonialist and the culturalist versions. The primordialist is an essentialist framework, assuming a foundational difference between Hindus and Muslims; these 'communities' "are viewed as bounded, homogeneous entities" (ibid: 37). Mayaram mentions another version of this approach, in 'cultural' terms, by Shashi Joshi and Bhagwan Joshi who argue that "the Muslim and non-Muslim lifeworlds are distinct and even contradictory....The cultural faultline can be accepted as a boundary not to be transgressed or tampered with" (quoted in Mayaram, 1997: 37). There is nothing natural or inevitable, according to Mayaram, about any 'ethnic closure' that may exist. One needs to examine such closures in terms of socio-political specificities of an ethnic community.

According to Mushirul Hasan, "Ordinary Muslims were not, as one is often led to believe, members of a monolithic community sitting sullenly apart, but were active participants in regional cultures whose perspective they shared" (1998: 16-17). In her intensive study, Mayaram questions the labelling of the Meo community variously as 'confused', 'syncretic' or 'imperfect' Muslims and prefers to use the notion of 'liminality', although with some hesitation, "given the absence of theoretic categories for people who are in-between and outside conventional categories" (1997: 38). The composite Muslim-Hindu culture of the Meo community, prior to its Islamization through the Tablighi movement, especially after the 1930-32 peasant movement in the princely states of Alwar and Bharatpur of the Rajputana region, may be termed by some as 'unique'. However, she points out that "a large number of groups in India have straddled this so-called 'faultline'. The *People of India* volumes of the Anthropological Survey of India, recently edited by K.S. Singh and his team, cite several hundred extant communities as lying between religions" (ibid: 47-48).

However, I would like to argue that, apart from the 'liminal' or 'in-between' cases, communities always share physical and social spaces. These shared spaces are essential in maintaining peace and harmony. 'Sharing' brings unity in diversity. On the other hand, an excessive 'celebration of diversity' tends to homogenize plurality and multi-vocality within communities and replaces porous and fuzzy borders by solid walls with other communities, breeding hatred, intolerance and violence. While referring to the situation in Bosnia, Mushirul Hasan states, "These Muslims, who were Yugoslavs just the other day, are now seen simply as Muslims. This often imparts a misleading ideological fixity to what is always a much more fluid and open-ended process of identity formation" (1998: 8-9). Describing the process of 'urbicide' as 'killing, slaughter or slaying of that which is urban' in Bosnia, Martin Coward (2002) shows how 'shared spaces' were systematically destroyed to make way for homogenization and separation of communities. He argues that "...the fundamental question for Bosnia is that of sharing a common space...The destruction of urban fabric is the destruction of precisely this common space and the attendant possibility of sharing such space. This is the logic of the destruction that is most dramatically highlighted in the collapse of the Stari Most..." (ibid: 32). One of the symbols of interaction and sharing was Stari Most or the Old (Ottoman) Bridge at Mostar, Bosnia-Herzegovina. It was destroyed on November 9, 1993. "Having survived natural disasters and wars, including shelling by the Bosnian Serb army in 1992, the bridge had finally been destroyed by Bosnian Croat forces intent on separating 'Muslim' east Mostar from 'Croat' west Mostar" (ibid: 29). The shared spaces were reconstituted through homogenization and ethnic cleansing. "A pattern emerged in the destruction of mosques. Typically, a mosque—despite its lack of strategic significance—would be targeted for shelling:

then after occupation of the town it would be dynamited, and in some cases the rubble was removed. In this way, the urban environment was ethnically cleansed. The physical traces of a multicultural history were removed, creating green fields, or car parks, in their wake" (ibid: 31). Similarly, neat lines, separating communities, which once lived together with shared traditions, have been drawn in different parts of the world. As Walker and Krishna, referring to the India-Pakistan partition state, "Today, that line is the site of more violent renegotiation. And elsewhere, in Sri Lanka, Bosnia, Rwanda, Palestine, indeed all over the planet, many more are drawn to the seductive allure of clean, precise lines that will forever separate *us* from *them*" (2002: 144).

T.K. Oommen (in this volume) makes a distinction between 'hegemonic' and 'emancipatory' cultural pluralisms. This is obviously to be understood as majoritarian and minority versions of cultural nationalism respectively. According to him, then, cultural nationalism of majority community is hegemonic whereas that of a minority community is emancipatory. However, it does not change the argument presented here. While agreeing that majoritarian cultural nationalism is almost always the initiator of exclusionist homogenization and ghettoization of minorities, we still have to consider who among the communities, both majority and minority, is interested in pushing the exclusionist agenda of violence and hatred.

Referring to the 'instrumentalist' perspective, Shail Mayaram mentions Paul Brass' contention that the "communalization of Muslim identity was a consequence of elite politics, which manipulated a following through the selection of divisive symbols" (1997: 18). Similarly, Majid Siddiqi "sees among the Meos a growing perception of an Islamic identity in the twentieth century due to the Tabligh (Faith) movement. The Meo movement is thereby appropriated by Islamic 'revivalism' " (1997: 94). Such approaches,

Mayaram argues, "superimpose a homogenization of motive on to the political action of culturally divergent groups and assume a passive populace until its 'awakening' by nationalism/communalism" (1997: 94).

Mohammad Ishaq Khan (1998) traces the Kashmir problem to the communalization of an essentially peasant question, in a way similar to Mayaram's analysis of the Meo situation. The problem starts, according to Khan, with the sale of Kashmir by the British to Gulab Singh, the Dogra Raja of Jammu, in 1846.

The Pandits in Kashmir dominated the social structure for centuries. They "were a tiny but not insignificant minority. Their numerical insignificance was overshadowed by their preponderance in the administration of the state under the Mughals (1586-1757), Afghans (1757-1819) and Sikhs (1819-46). They were so well entrenched that the Dogra rulers found it impossible to displace them" (Khan, 1998: 202). On the other hand, the peasants and other groups at lower rungs were gradually absorbed into Islam under the influence of Sufi missionaries. "Under the inspiring leadership of Shaikh Nuruddin Rishi (1379-1442) and a host of his disciples dispersed in every nook and corner of the valley, Kashmiri folk—agriculturalists, artisans and boatmen—gradually assimilated Islam through a process of acculturation during the fifteenth to eighteenth centuries" (ibid: 202). The Dogra rule, since 1846, created a landed aristocracy, mainly of Kashmiri Pandits and Dogra Rajputs. This, in turn, violated the traditional proprietary rights of the peasants, reducing them to 'virtual serfdom'. The elites and pan-Islamic movements, in order to redefine the identity orientation of a community, frequently appropriated such conditions of large-scale deprivation. Maulana Abdus Salam Hamdani, writing in August, 1931, lamented that "...the Muslim subjects of Kashmir were greatly oppressed. There was nothing communal in this agitation and it was a pity that some people were trying to give a communal colour" (quoted in

Khan, 1998: 217, footnote 75). Similarly, Mushirul Hasan (1998) argues that the themes of dissatisfaction and dispossession have been used for mustering support for a 'singular identity'. "This is invariably done in South Asia, a region marked by economic disparities and social diversities, to capture power or demand more active redistribution. In such situations, economic and power interests of the dominant strata of the group get camouflaged, submerged in, or blended with the passions of identity of particular communities and castes" (ibid: 10-11).

The Muslim elite of Srinagar also raised the demand for singular identity in the 1920s. "...the city contained the wealthiest and most articulate section of Muslims, the Naqshbandis, the Shawls and the Shahdads. While the Naqshbandis had large landed estates in the Valley and had also been the leading merchants, the Shawls and the Shahdads had a monopoly of the carpet and shawl trade in Kashmir....They not only demanded a larger representation of Muslims in government services and an improvement in the condition of Muslim education in the state, but also the grant of proprietary rights in land to the peasants, and abolition of the hated corvees. This shows that middle class leaders wanted to utilize the support of the masses for the furtherance of their demands" (Khan, 1998: 214).

But responses to conditions of 'dissatisfaction and dispossession' are not necessarily univocal. There have always been reformist voices to improve the conditions of the community. In Kashmir, "the Muslim education movement was started in the 1890s by Mir Waiz Maulvi Ghulam Rasool Shah to safeguard against Muslims being driven towards Christianity. He believed that education on Western lines, supported by Koranic teachings, would produce young Muslims of capacity and character...Interestingly enough, the local Muslims under the leadership of fanatic *mullahs* raised a violent agitation and attempts were made on the life of the Maulvi" (ibid: 210). But, the voices of 'Kashmiri nation' and 'Kashmiriyat', with shared spaces for Hindus and Muslims, remained prominent, especially after the creation of All Jammu and Kashmir National Conference in 1939.

Shail Mayaram's analysis of the Meos is, however, more sophisticated. She argues that (1) the agrarian unrest of 1932 among the Meo peasants of Alwar and Bharatpur states of Rajputana preceded the serious efforts of Islamization by the Tablighi movement of Maulana Ilyas. Therefore, the Meo movement of 1932 cannot be seen to have been appropriated by Islamic 'revivalism', as is viewed by some historians. A Meo peasant movement was declared as a 'Muslim' movement, preparing the ground for both Hindu and Muslim ethnic mobilizers to 'exploit' the situation. (2) "Rather than attribute the Meo movement to a pre-existing divide or to Islamic education...sectarian conflict can be ascribed to the exclusivist 'Hinduization' of the Alwar and Bharatpur states..." (Mayaram, 1997: 272). Shraddhanand's 'Shuddhi' movement was paralleled by Ilyas's Tablighi movement. The latter was intensified after large-scale state violence against the Meos during the 1930s and even more after the Partition violence against the 'Muslim' Meos. (3) Thus, the 'liminality' of Meo community, deeply embedded in regional culture, was sought to be destroyed by ethnic mobilizers, assisted by 'print capitalism'. "The lithographic press, available to various nationalisms, made possible the reproduction of homogenized social identities that overwrote difference" (ibid: 273). However, Meo agency cannot be disregarded and they continue to resist attempts to transform Meo culture into a sanitized, homogenous, urban model of Islam.

Thus, on the one hand, if the liberal democratic state is considered to perform violence by denying the role of culturally embedded plural identities in favour of homogenized equal citizenship, then, on the other hand, the existence of a diversity of hostile and homogenized communities is no reason for celebration either. In such a case, neither majoritarian nor minority ethno-nationalist movements are emancipatory in nature. Such movements deny the existence of shared life-worlds. Simultaneously, these movements are not egalitarian in ideology and are, in fact, reactionary, totalitarian and oppressive in the name of 'tradition'. As Mayaram argues, "Individual identity involves negotiating with competing systems of collective representations. It involves very different responses, as each restructures and reshapes his/her lifeworld. What Meo narratives suggest is the plurality of identity in which space and time figure as contingent categories. They indicate also the failure of binary categories of understanding...to express the diversity of felt, lived existence" (ibid: 277-78).

The complexity and contingent character of 'Muslim' identities, always in the making, like all other identities, is compellingly demonstrated by Nathalie Clayer and Alexandre Popovic by examining various ethnic layers in the Balkans during the post-Ottoman period:

> The Muslim communities living in the Balkans were formed during the long Ottoman rule extending from a hundred and fifty to five hundred years, depending on the region, from the late fourteenth to the early twentieth century. These communities were formed after Turkish (or Turkish speaking) immigrants from Anatolia settled in the Balkans, other non-Turkish speaking Muslims (e.g., Tatars, Tcherkesses, etc.) migrated, and the local population in regions like Bosnia-Herzegovina, Albania, Crete, Macedonia, Bulgaria and Greece became Islamized.
>
> At the end of the Ottoman rule, which occurred at very different times in different regions (between 1699 and 1912), these communities—or at least what remained of them after the fairly large-scale migration—found themselves living with the surrounding Christian (and other) communities in

> the following nation-states: Romania, Bulgaria, Yugoslavia, Greece and Albania...they have lost the privileged status they enjoyed during the Ottoman period (Clayer and Popovic, 1998: 405).

These 'Muslims' carried with themselves layers of different identities. Language is one of the most influential of shared aspects of a group of people. It is central to the world of meanings, and therefore, to culture. In this sense, Muslims shared so much with other communities.

> ...just as the Muslims of Bosnia-Herzegovina share their language with the Serbs and Croats, the Albanians Muslims speak the same language as their Catholic and Orthodox compatriots. In addition to political factors which were generally underestimated, language was one of the main vehicles which led to an Albanian state and nation (ibid: 414-15).

If language brought different religious groups together, there were several 'dividing lines' within religious groups.

> If one goes back to the end of the Ottoman period when there was no border separating the Albanian Muslims from one another, they were still far from being a homogeneous group. The most important 'dividing line' was between the Sunnis and the Bektachis. The latter belonged to a tarikat, a mystic Muslim brotherhood from Central Anatolia who followed an extremely heterodox and syncretic doctrine.... Other more or less visible 'dividing lines' were created by various peculiarities: ethnic peculiarities (between two Albanian ethnic sub-groups—the Gregs in the north, in Kosovo and in the major portion of Macedonia, and the Tosks in the south); regional peculiarities (in the Dibra regions, for example); and peculiarities related to clans (in the mountains in the north of the present Albania), without forgetting the social disparities (from the beys who were big

landlords to the shepherds in the mountains and the officials in the Ottoman Government) (ibid: 415-16).

The above description would not be much different for the Muslims in India. Nor would it be different for the Hindus in India. Who, then, transform these layers of diversity into singular, homogenous, religious identities? What kind of ethnic mobilizers gain from such transformations? And, do the people at large passively receive these ideologies of homogenization and hatred and ethnic cleansing? People challenge, contest and negotiate with such forces but may not always succeed.

This was the situation at the time of the bloody violence at the time of India's partition. Violence fed still greater violence. Perfectly normal neighbours suddenly turned hostile and suspicious. Urvashi Butalia sums up the homogenization process in a village in Rawalpindi district: "...in 1947, the population of Thoa [Khalsa] had been mostly Sikh. But now, there wasn't a single Sikh left there. Instead, they had been replaced by Muslims, many of whom must have carried their own tales of violence at the hands of Hindus and Sikhs" (Butalia, 2002: 160). Butalia goes on to describe the recent 'journey for peace and reconciliation' made by Bir Bahadur Singh from India to his 'home' in Rawalpindi where he grew up. There were no faultlines between Sikhs and Muslims. The faultlines were the constructions of the ethnic mobilizers who wished to exercise power over homogenized diversities, setting aside the material well-being of ordinary folk.

Just as the 'Hindutva' forces flash the banner of 'authentic' Hinduism, so do the Muslim mobilizers and homogenizers deny the diversity and pluralism within 'Muslim communities'. Pointing out that 'true Islam' has always been a matter of dispute, whose outcome (always temporary) has been bound up with power, Joya Chatterji concludes that "there is no 'authentic' soul or spirit of Islam, or indeed of the Muslim community". From her standpoint, "authenticity can only be a fundamentalist claim that seeks to standardize, essentialize and sentimentalize a past which has been characterized by plurality, multivocality and bitter conflict" (quoted in Hasan, 1998: 12). The diversity of shared cultures does not threaten secular nationalism and, therefore, need not be seen as antagonistic to it. Indeed, "the problem of identity in South Asia has been more complex and nuanced than permitted by the protagonists of the 'two-nation' theory of the practitioners of a historiography based on a *binary opposition between secular nationalism and religious nationalism*' (Bose and Jalal-Ayesha, quoted in Hasan, 1998: 16). People have shared social spaces in the past and continue to do so. This is an essential ingredient for a healthy, vibrant and pluralist democratic society. People need to assert their right to continue to live in shared spaces and ensure that "their sane and sober voices should not be stifled by the weight of *Muslim orthodoxy, Hindu revivalism and the Orientalist discourse*" (ibid: 19).

Engaging with the Orientalist discourse in her critical introduction to post-colonial theory, which is "situated somewhere in the interstices between Marxism and post-modernism/post-structuralism", Leela Gandhi evaluates various explanations of anti-Western nationalisms of the 'Third World'. In this context, she disagrees with Hobsbawm for whom "the characteristic nationalist movements of the late twentieth century are essentially negative, or rather divisive...(They are mostly) rejections of modern modes of political organization, both national and supranational. Time and again they seem to be reactions of weakness and fear, attempts to erect barricades to keep at bay the forces of the modern world" (Hobsbawm, 1990 quoted in Gandhi, 1999: 107-8). While arguing against the view that Third World nationalism is a 'derivative discourse' and that there is 'good' nationalism (Western) and 'bad' nationalism (Third World), she, nevertheless, recognizes the violent consequences of the 'rhetoric of particularism' of various new nationalisms.

"Nothing in the preceding discussion is meant to condone the horrific violence justified in the name of nationalism. East or West, we are now aware of the xenophobia, racism and loathing which attend the rhetoric of particularism. Nationalism has become the popular pretext for contemporary disquisitions of intolerance, separating Croatians and Serbians, Greeks and Macedonians, Estonians and Russians, Slovaks and Czechs, Armenians and Azerbaijanis, Israelis and Palestinians, Hindus and Muslims" (ibid: 108). But, of course, one has to agree with her that "it is important to recognize that forms of nationalism which refuse the singular content of modernity are not necessarily all designed to turn human beings against each other" (ibid: 110).

Post-modernist 'celebration of diversity' on the one hand and Leftist concern for 'global solidarities' against institutionalized suffering and disparities on the other present a tension, with the 'post-nationalist' turn in post-colonial theory. Explaining this, Leela Gandhi takes off from a clash between various forms of humanism and anti-humanism:

> 'Humanism' is a highly contentious term....These various humanisms are, however, unified in their belief that underlying the diversity of human experience it is possible, first, to discern a universal and given human nature, and secondly to find it revealed in the common language of rationality. In defence of this belief, Marxist exponents of humanistic principles, such as Noam Chomsky, Fredric Jameson and Jurgen Habermas have argued that humanism holds out the possibility of a rational and universal consensus between responsible individuals with regard to the conceptualisation of a humane, progressive and just social order. In contrast, poststructuralist and postmodernist anti-humanists maintain that any universal or normative postulation of rational unanimity is totalitarian and hostile to the challenges of otherness and difference (Gandhi, 1999: 27).

This creates a difference in the understanding of the possibilities of communication between diverse groups, communities, nations or civilizations. "Political mobilisation and ethical principles, as Marxist critics forcefully argue, necessarily require some sort of cross-cultural consensus. For a postmodern thinker like Lyotard, however, the very process of reaching consensus is vitiated by a 'conversational imperialism'... postcolonial studies critics are left to ponder the apparent chasm between the poststructuralist insistence on the impossibility of a universal human nature and the opposing Marxist verdict on the impossibility of a politics which lacks the principle of 'solidarity' " (ibid: 27-28).

Terry Eagleton, in a critque of post-modernist distancing away from emancipatory political agenda, "sees postmodernism as a form of 'culturalism' because it refuses to recognize that what different ethnic groups have in common socially and politically is more important to their emancipation than their cultural differences... (and that) postmodernism's glamorization of the 'marginal' and suspicion of centers of power and authority forbids it conceiving of a majority political movement" (quoted in Sim, 2001: 235). Similarly, as H. Bhabha writes, arguing against the celebration of frozen identities from the past, Fanon "is far too aware of the dangers of the fixity and fetishism of identities within the calcification of colonial culture to recommend that 'roots' be struck in the celebratory romance of the past" (1994: 9). Despite the need for 'psychological and cultural rehabilitation' during the anti-colonial struggles, for Fanon, "aggressive assertions of cultural identity frequently come in the way of wider international solidarities" (Gandhi, 1999: 123).

'Celebration of differences' is also a means of mobilizing the 'subaltern energies' in the service of dominant layers of a 'community'. In such cases, the demands for preserving cultural differences "seek to legitimize existing power relations and forms of subordination. In fact, such claims ignore the inequalities that prevail within the community" (Mahajan, 1998: 11). Similarly, Gandhi states that "multicultural celebrations of 'cultural diversity' conveniently disguise rather more serious economic and political disparities" (1999: 136).

The staunch critics of post-colonial theorization, Arif Dirlik (1994) and Aijaz Ahmad (1995) also insist on the need for collective politics based on ground reality in opposition to "a carnivalesque collapse and play of identities" in post-colonial writing (see Gandhi, 1999: 56-63 on the role of post-colonial intellectuals and the explosion of 'marginality studies'). However, it would be inappropriate to disregard the significance of 'cultural identities' altogether and reduce the entire question of 'international solidarities' to one of 'classes'.

Here, a brief engagement with Habermas' notion of 'public sphere' may be useful. As Douglas Kellner summarizes the position, "Habermas describes a transition from the liberal public sphere which originated in the Enlightenment and the American and French Revolution to a media-dominated public sphere in the current era of what he calls 'welfare state capitalism and mass democracy'. This historical transformation is grounded...in Horkheimer and Adorno's analysis of the culture industry, in which giant corporations have taken over the public sphere and transformed it from a sphere of rational debate into one of manipulative consumption and passivity" (n.d.). But, there are problems with this formulation of idealized 'bourgeois public sphere' "when in fact certain groups were excluded and participation was thus limited". Kellner argues that "while the concept of the public sphere and democracy assume a liberal and populist celebration of diversity, tolerance, debate, and consensus, in actuality, the bourgeois public sphere was dominated by white, property-owning males" (ibid). In fact, there were several 'oppositional and non-bourgeois public spheres' whose existence Habermas ignores. Interestingly, as Mary Ryan (1992) notes, "not only did Habermas neglect women's public spheres, but marks the decline of the public sphere precisely at the moment when women were beginning to get political power and become actors" (quoted in Kellner, n.d.).

In India, today, separate oppositional public spheres are emerging while the extent of violence in the civil society is increasing in an unstable political environment, notwithstanding Atul Kohli's commitment to the 'success of Indian democracy'. Looking into the cases of instability in Africa, Rajen Harshe states: "Amin relates the phenomenon of the rise of ethnicity to the disintegration of the ruling classes. Basically, Amin argues that the movements built round ethnicity have the potential to break up the power base as also the unity of the ruling classes" (2002: 1408). Whether the ethnic mobilizations have the potential to break up the unity of the ruling classes or not, such mobilizations, with new oppositional public spheres, appear to emerge when there is a realignment or displacement of ruling classes and consequent political instability. Displacement of upper castes and almost the disappearance of big landlords after the independence, and the emergence of the power bloc of aggressive rich peasants from the intermediate castes in almost all the states of India have provided the cultural and political environment for large-scale caste-based mobilization, leading to new fragmentary politics. The emerging fragmentary, oppositional public spheres are simultaneously emancipatory and regressive.

Take the case of politics in Uttar Pradesh. According to Sudha Pai:

> During the 1990s, UP has held three assembly and four Lok Sabha elections. It is widely accepted that these elections, held against the background of rising levels of awareness among the lower castes of their disadvantaged socio-economic status, played a salient role in accelerating

> the process of democratization and identity assertion against upper caste domination. The spread of the electoral process into backward regions where dalits were not allowed to vote earlier and the appointment of Mayavati, a dalit woman, as chief minister in a socially conservative state was of great symbolic importance providing dalits with self-confidence... However, the relentless pursuit of identity politics and religious mobilisation based on Hindutva for over a decade has created fragmentation rather than a stable multi-party system as was expected in a post-Congress polity in UP.
>
> As a result, all the major political parties in UP exhibit a number of unhealthy traits today that are not conducive to the development of a stable party system or government. Closely identified with specific ethnic groups—the BJP with the upper castes, the SP with the backward (castes) and the BSP with the lower castes—they have become narrow sectarian formations, which having reached a plateau are frustrated in their search for political power (2002: 1335).

Thus, the 'emancipatory' mobilization of the dalits in Uttar Pradesh simultaneously prevents ideology-based larger solidarities. Similarly, Surinder Jodhka informs that 'dissociation, distancing and autonomy' are "used as strategies of social and cultural assertion by the dalits in rural Punjab" (2002: 1822). This homogenized fragmentation, while it does play a critical role in increasing awareness of marginalized communities, has its limitations in creating possibilities of social and economic transformation. What, in fact, is emerging is an unprincipled politics. In Uttar Pradesh, increasing ethnic mobilization has not resulted in a transparent, vibrant public sphere. On the other hand, one sees an opportunistic, manipulative personalized politics of nepotism, allurements and shifting loyalties, devoid of any ideology. As Pai argues, "the fragmented social profile of voters has led to the proliferation of parties, groups, or individual leaders who are not bound by any ideology except the desire for personal political power and sectional benefits which has become the normative framework of the political class in the state" (2002: 1335). Not only that, all major political parties in Uttar Pradesh send a significant number of criminals as members of the Legislative Assembly. Neither the issue of 'intra-group inequalities' within 'ethnic communities' nor the one about political consolidation in to 'larger solidarities' receive any attention.

In a recent article, Yoginder Sikand presents a subaltern, oppositional representation of Islam, which is building alliances with marginalized non-Muslim groups like the dalits, tribals and some of the other backward castes. "If elite Muslim understandings of Islam tend to focus on memories of Muslim grandeur, subaltern understandings tend....to stress Islam as a force for social justice and liberation from oppression" (Sikand, 2002: 3849). Sikand's analysis is based on Muslims writings in Bangalore-based English fortnightly *Dalit Voice.* "These growing voices of protest are directed both internally, at the 'ulama and the ashraf elite', as well as externally, at upper caste Hindus, both of whom are seen as complicit in the oppression of the Muslim masses" (ibid: 3857).

It is such non-exclusionist, non-homogenizing, voices that can expand the shared spaces in society and thus build a foundation for a violence-free pluralist democracy, with a vibrant and transparent public sphere.

References

Ahmad, A. 1995. "The Politics of Literary Postcoloniality", *Race and Class*, 36 (3): 1-20.

Bhabha, H. 1994. *The Location of Culture*, London: Routledge.

Butalia, Urvashi. 2002. "A Necessary Journey: A Story of Friendship and Reconciliation", *Alternatives*, 27: 147-64.

Calhoun, Craig. (ed.). 1992. *Habermas and the Public Sphere.* Cambridge: The MIT Press.

Clayer, Nathalie and Alexandre, Popovic. "Muslim Identity in the Balkans in the post-Ottoman Period", in Mushirul Hasan, 1998: 405-23.

Coward, Martin. 2002. "Community as Heterogeneous Ensemble: Mostar and Multiculturalism", *Alternatives* 27: 29-66.

Dirlik, A. 1994. "The Postcolonial Aura: Third World Criticism in the Age of Global Capitalism", *Critical Inquiry*, 20: 328-56.

Gandhi, Leela. 1999. *Postcolonial Theory: A Critical Introduction*, Delhi: Oxford University Press.

Harshe, Rajen. 2002. "Marxism, Capitalism, Globalisation", *Economic and Political Weekly*, XXXVII (15): 1407-12.

Hasan, Mushirul. (ed.). 1998. *Islam, Communities and the Nation: Muslim Identities in South Asia and Beyond*, New Delhi: Manohar.

Jodhka, Surinder S. 2002. "Caste and Untouchability in Rural Punjab", *Economic and Political Weekly*, XXXVII (19): 1813-23.

Karam, Azza M. 2000. "Islamisms and the decivilising processes of globalisation", in Alberto Arce and Norman Long (eds.), *Anthropology, Development and Modernities: Exploring Discourses, Counter-Tendencies and Violence*, London: Routledge.

Kellner, Douglas. n.d. *Habermas, the Public Sphere, and Democracy: A Critical Intervention*, (http://gseis.ucla.edu/faculty/kellner/habermas.htm).

Khan, Mohammad Ishaq. "Kashmiri Muslims: Social and Identity Consciousness", in Mushirul Hasan, 1998: 201-28.

Mahajan, Gurpreet. (ed.). 1998. *Democracy, Difference and Social Justice*, New Delhi: Oxford University Press.

Mayaram, Shail. 1997. *Resisting Regimes: Myth, Memory and the Shaping of A Muslim Identity*, New Delhi: Oxford University Press.

Momin, A.R. 2002. "Celebrating Diversity", *Sociological Bulletin*, 55 (1): 101-15.

Pai, Sudha. 2002. "Electoral Identity Politics in Uttar Pradesh: Hung Assembly Again", *Economic and Political Weekly*, XXXVII (14): 1334-41.

Parekh, Bhikhu. 2000. *Rethinking Multiculturalism: Cultural Diversity and Political Theory*. London: Macmillan.

Ryan, Mary. 1992. "Gender and Public Access: Women's Politics in Nineteenth Century America," in Calhoun, 1992: 259-88.

Sikand, Yoginder. 2002. "Islamic Perspectives on Liberation and Dialogue in Contemporary India: Muslim Writings in Dalit Voice", *Economic and Political Weekly*, XXXVII (37): 3849-58.

Sim, Stuart. (ed.). 2001. *The Routledge Companion to Postmodernism*, London: Routledge.

6

Culture and Violence

Explaining Reasons for Action

PARAMJIT S. JUDGE

It is generally assumed that the individuals join a particular movement, because they share the ideology inherent in it. Ideology acquires importance when a movement exhibits two distinctive features, that is, it uses violence as a means, and it is organized. Writers on social movements argue that all social movements have a degree of organization (Hebrele, 1949; Rao, 1978). Largely depending upon the ideology and interest that has been articulated by its leaders the degree of organization varies among the movements. An organized movement assumes the presence of ideologically committed leaders. In the modern world the movements rarely emerge spontaneously. Rather, they are organized consciously keeping in mind the objectives or changes the leaders intend or propose to bring about in the existing state of affairs (Blumer, 1957). For consciously waged movements the ideology becomes central in their entire conduct.

A movement in general does not appeal to all the members of the society to join it. In fact, there is always a discriminatory approach that a movement entails, because by virtue of its ideology and the change it aspires to bring about, it enters into conflict with certain sections of the society. In this regard, the means employed by the movement acquire a significant place. The leaders, in general, conduct the movements in a civil society within the framework of legality. In the case of such kinds of movements, which are legal and non-violent, the ideology of the movement and that of the participants tends to overlap. Moreover, the civil society has an institutional mechanism to handle dissent and change. All movements, however, do not remain confined to the legal framework. Rather, some use extra-legal means to achieve their objectives.

Certain objectives of a movement may come into direct conflict with the state, as they cannot be achieved within the framework of law. The legitimacy and appeal of such movements lie in the ideology. In general, the ideology involves the lofty ideals of achieving equality, bringing heaven on earth, or attaining salvation by following the path of a particular prophet.[1] Liberation from colonial rule or end of discrimination against a minority could be the ideological basis of the movements that do not adopt legal means to achieve their objectives. Generally, the value-oriented movements, to use Smelser's (1961) typology, have tendency to use extra-legal means to achieve their objectives. In a way the ideological basis of a movement is the major reason for its using extra-legal means, which further depends upon both how a political system has defined the legal framework and the interaction between the movement and the state. More lofty the ideals, more are the chances of occurrence of violence in a movement.

This paper, which is based on a study conducted by this author, aims at explaining reasons for the participants to join two violent movements that occurred in Punjab, namely, the Naxalite movement and the Khalistan movement. Both these movements were committed to the use of violence for achieving their objectives though ideologically they were different from each other. The Naxalite movement had all-India character, whereas the Khalistan movement was confined to Punjab only. However, in terms of acts of violence, the Khalistan movement turned global as a result of the activities of the Sikh diaspora in the Western countries. The bombing of the Air India plane—Kanishka—further demonstrates the international reach of the Khalistan movement. Both the movements used terror as their major weapon. Before the discussion of certain salient features of these movements, it is worthwhile to make general observations on terrorist methods.

For the present purpose, terrorist method is defined as an act of violence, the aim of which is to create fear in the minds of the defined opponent (Thorton, 1964; Wilkinson, 1977).[2] Thus, terrorist method entails four features. First, it is a conscious and organized use of violence. Not only that, it is a deliberately planned act of violence. Second, it has a discriminatory character in the sense that the actors choose a particular set of people as their targets sharing certain common features, such as religion, economic or political position. Third, it is a tactics of a movement to create fear among the opponents. It generally happens when the movement is weak and it wants to create an impact larger than it can normally do. Terrorist methods cannot succeed in achieving the goal of the movement, but it may be successful in making the cause known to all and in drawing the attention of the possible recruits. Fourth, the terrorist acts, such as hijacking and killings, are carefully selected so that they have a dramatic effect. It is also observed that one of the purposes of the terrorist actions is to force the regime to enact suppressive laws so that it loses its legitimacy in the eyes of the people. A movement aiming at achieving such an end is active in a society that has not yet fully developed its institutional bases. However, this objective also suggests that the participants of the violent movement are not mindless killers. Rather, they are educated and ideologically articulate individuals and they have chosen terrorist methods out of their convictions (Steinhoff, 1976; Russell and Miller, 1985). To qualify this observation, it should be added that it may not hold true for all kinds of violent movements, particularly the educational level of the participants may vary with their position in the organizational hierarchy.

The main conjecture of the paper is that it is not necessary that the participants in a militant movement, which uses terrorist methods as the major weapon of struggle, join it due to their ideological commitments. However, their reasons for joining the movement may be understood in the context of the social, cultural and economic dimensions of the society. In the light of this argument the discussion in this paper has been divided into four parts. The first part deals with the Naxalite movement, whereas in the second the Khalistan movement has been described with a view to succinctly examine the ideology and practice of both the movements. In the third part the social background of the participants and their reasons for joining the movements have been discussed. It is worthwhile to inform that the author has collected the data by using interview method. In the last part of the paper an attempt has been made to analyze those reasons for joining the movements, which may not be inherently linked with the ideological appeal of each movement.

I
Naxalite Movement

The Naxalite movement originated from West Bengal in 1967 and within two years it spread to most of the parts of the country, particularly the rural areas. It was primarily a communist movement, which was aimed at bringing about people's democratic revolution in India. The movement emerged out of the dispute between the pro-Soviet Union and pro-China communists over the path of India's socialist revolution. Both the then existing communist parties, namely, Communist Party of India (CPI) and the Communist Party of India-Marxists (CPI-M), had adopted the parliamentary path to socialism. The Maoist cadres in the CPI-M were unhappy with the party over this issue. In 1967, the CPI-M became the partner in the coalition government in West Bengal. In the villages, which fall under the Naxalbari police station in the Darjeeling district, the Maoist leaders organized the forcible occupation of land and crops of the landlords. The police undertook stern measures against the people of the area who were mainly the Santhal tribals. The tribals retaliated as a result of which a police inspector was killed. This led to massive suppressive measures of the police in which some tribals including women lost their lives (Judge, 1992).

There was nothing unique about this event as such occurrences were not unusual in the simmering Indian villages where the landordism had been dominant. However, the fact that the peasant agitation was suppressed so violently when the representative party of the workers and peasants was ruling partner in the state created tremendous resentment within the party. The pro-Mao communists started leaving the CPI-M, whereas some were expelled. All these communists got organized and constituted a co-ordination committee, which in 1969 was turned into the third communist party of India, namely, the Communist Party of India-Marxists Leninists (CPI-ML). The new party declared "Chinese path is our path". Strategically, the revolutionary struggle would involve protracted warfare in which the revolution would start from the villages and ultimately the cities would be encircled.

The CPI-ML identified the conflict between the big landowner and the landless peasant as the main contradiction in the Indian society. The Indian bourgeoisie was treated with contempt, because it was regarded as comprador in character without any autonomy. The People's Democratic Revolution, which was visualized by this party, was to be achieved through armed struggle and the parliamentary path was considered counter-revolutionary. All this was a typical Maoist point of view that was articulated by the CPI-ML. They did not hide their liking for the Chinese path of revolution as it was epitomized by its slogan "Chinese path is our path and Chinese chairman is our chairman". Charu Mazumdar emerged as the leader of the Naxalite movement. Though there was an overemphasis on the Chinese path and the writings of Mao Tse-Tung, yet the Naxalite movement approached the revolution from the perspective of people and their organizations in India. From this perspective it was an insurrectionary movement. Interestingly, the Naxalite movement was the first of its kind in India, because it spread all over the country and overcame the caste, religious and regional barriers.

The mass insurrectionary approach of the Naxalite movement did not last long. Within few months of its formation Charu Mazumdar gave a new tactical line, generally known as the line of 'annihilation of class enemies'. It transformed the movement into a kind of terrorist movement, as in the light of this line the mass organizations were regarded as counter-revolutionary and were disbanded. The guerrilla squads were to work in total secrecy. The identification of the class enemies would also be carried out through whisper campaign. The revolutionary would go to poor peasant and ask him whether that particular landlord should be eliminated. Later on, Charu Mazumdar also argued for the use of the conventional weapons like sickle, javelin, axe etc. to kill the class enemies. Such weapons were easier to carry from one place to another and there was no fear of their being detected. The annihilation of class enemies would lead to the elimination of the oppressor, which would mobilize the masses. The notion of 'red terror' was used to explain the fear the annihilation of landlords would create among the enemies. They would flee to the cities and the rural areas would be liberated from the class enemies. The cumulative effect of this tactical line would be the liberation of village from enemies. In the end, the cities would be encircled to give the deathblow to the feudal-comprador bourgeoisie to usher in the People's Democratic Revolution.

The Naxalite movement in Punjab began in reaction to the events that occurred in Naxalbari. Punjab had a tradition of the communist movement. Thus, the presence of the pro-China communists in Punjab was no surprise. They left the CPI-M and joined the new movement. After the CPI-ML was formed, the Punjab Maoists established the state unit of the party and they implemented the line of annihilation of class enemies in the state. Organizationally, they got divided and by the end of 1969 there were three factions of the Naxalites. Two of them implemented the official line of the party. In comparison with other states of India, Punjab was agriculturally the most developed state. The green revolution had already taken off in the state. The emergence and denouement of the Naxalite movement in Punjab had certain distinct features from those of other states like Bihar, West Bengal and Andhra Pradesh where the movement became strong (Banerjee, 1980). However, the actual life span of the movement in Punjab shared the same phases with the rest of the country. Dasgupta (1974) has identified the following phases of the Naxalite movement:

1. Naxalbari uprisings and reaction of the Maoist cadres to the event.
2. The period between the Naxalbari uprisings and the formation of the CPI-ML. During this period the Maoist formed a co-ordination committee, namely, All India Co-ordination Committee of Communist Revolutionaries (AICCCR). Charu Mazumdar emerged as undisputed leader of the movement. During this period, a series of mass struggles in various states including Punjab were organized.
3. The CPI-ML was formed in 1969 and it organized various struggles. The line of annihilation of class enemies was implemented all over India.
4. The movement shifted to the urban areas without any change in the tactics. However, this shift was a strategic retreat of the CPI-ML as the cities were to be the last to be captured in the People's Democratic Revolution.

5. In July 1972, Charu Mazumdar was arrested and he died in the police custody due to cardiac arrest from whereon began the dissipation of the movement.

During the Naxalite movement, a total of 73 attempts were made to annihilate the class enemies in Punjab, out of which seven remained unsuccessful. In the real or fake encounters with the police 82 Naxalites were killed. In Punjab, the movement continued till the imposition of emergency in 1975 by the then Prime Minister, Indira Gandhi. Between 1972 and 1975, the militant posture at the levels of practice as well as rhetoric was maintained (Judge, 2000). The movement had lost its effectiveness in 1977 and from the next year a new movement surfaced that slowly emerged as the most powerful terrorist movement ever experienced in Punjab. All the democratic processes were sidelined after 1983. Jarnail Singh Bhindranwala climbed up as the leader of the movement and after 1984, when he was killed in the army attack at the Golden Temple at Amritsar, inspired the movement as a legend and became more lethal in his effect.

II
Khalistan Movement

Ideologically, the Khalistan movement was qualitatively different from the Naxalite movement. The Naxalite movement was aimed at the transformation of the relations of production to bring about equality among human beings. Conversely, the Khalistan movement had the objective of the attainment of Khalistan—an independent sovereign state for Sikhs. For the leaders of the Naxalite movement religion was the opium of the masses, whereas religion was primary in the conduct of affairs of the Khalistan movement. However, both were value-oriented movements and believed in and practised violent methods to achieve their respective goals. During the high tide of the Khalistan movement, the Punjab Naxalites remained divided in their views on the movement. A section of

Naxalites supported the Khalistan movement on grounds of the right to self-determination for a nationality (ibid). However, a majority of the Naxalite groups was critical of the movement and confronted it by organizing their own fighting squad when the Khalistani militants began killing some prominent Naxalite leaders. It may be noted that in terms of the killings by both the militants and police and army in Punjab the Khalistan movement cannot be compared with any of the kind in the state. When the movement was suppressed, about 25,000 people had lost their lives due to it (Puri and Judge, 2000).

The Khalistan movement may broadly be divided into six distinct phases.[3] The first phase may be characterized as the period of the latent conflict when various social, economic, political and religious factors began to converge to create forces that produced manifest conflict. All this happened in the 1970s when both covert as well as overt developments took place that led to the mobilization of the Sikhs for autonomy and distinct identity. The Akali Dal contributed through the passing of the Anandpur Sahib Resolution in 1973. Sant Kartar Singh Bhindranwala toured Punjab in order to homogenize the Sikh identity through the Khalsa forum. In the process he also generated anti-Nirankari wave. There was an organization of radical Sikhs, like Dal Khalsa, which articulated the glory and autonomy of the Sikhs. There were also non-resident Indian Sikhs who openly talked about the desire for the creation of Khalistan. The Congress and the Akali Dal—the two major political parties—competed with each other for capturing the votes of the Sikhs.

The second phase began when all these developments combined in a strange way to result into the violent clash at Amritsar between the adherents of Sant Nirankari Sect and the followers of Sant Jarnail Singh Bhindranwala, the head of the Damdami Taksal, on 13 April 1978. This resulted in the killing of 13 followers of Bhindranwala and three Nirankaris. This incident tended to serve both legitimacy and excuse for armed attacks on the Nirankaris including the murder of its chief, Baba Gurbachan Singh, in 1980. Sant Jarnail Singh Bhindranwala participated in the elections of the Shiromani Gurdwara Prabandhak Committee (SGPC) in 1979 in which he was marginalized. It is alleged that the Congress party supported him in this venture. The murder of the chief editor of *Punjab Kesari* group of newspapers, Lala Jagat Narain, as well as the arrest and then release of the Sant Bhindranwala, were the major events of the year 1980. The Akali Dal-led government in the state had been dismissed by the Prime Minister Indira Gandhi and the Congress government with Darbara Singh as the Chief Minister following fresh elections was formed in 1980. In November 1983, Darbara Singh-led government was dismissed when the Hindu bus passengers were killed and the President's rule was imposed. Extensive fortification of the entire Golden Temple Complex was done under the direction of General Shahbeg Singh. It was Sant Jarnail Singh Bhindranwala who virtually ruled over Punjab through his campaign of violence (Puri, Judge and Sekhon, 1999).

The third phase started with 'Operation Blue Star' in June 1984 for the purpose of flushing out terrorists. The fierce battle that raged inside the Golden Temple Complex resulted in significant loss of life and extensive destruction of the Akal Takhat. The Sant Bhindranwala and his close aides were killed. However, the army strike at this most sacred place of the Sikhs led to a widespread feeling of hurt and anger. There was a revolt in the Sikh Regiments of the Indian Army too.

The post-Operation Blue Star happenings further alienated the Sikhs from the Indian State. On October 31, 1984, Prime Minister Indira Gandhi was assassinated by her Sikh bodyguards and in reaction to that thousands of innocent Sikhs were killed in riots that followed in Delhi, Kanpur and many other places. By the end of the year 1984, when Rajiv Gandhi became the Prime Minister, the situation seemed to have reached the extreme level of hostility of the Sikh community towards the Indian government.

As the dialogue between Sant Harchand Singh Longowal and the Prime Minister began and culminated into the Rajiv-Longowal Accord in July 1985, the fourth phase began with a hope. The restoration of the democratic process raised hopes of a possible solution to the Punjab problem. The Accord faced its first jolt when Sant Longowal was shot dead by the terrorists within a month of its signing. The central government failed to honour the Accord, as the city of Chandigarh was not transferred to Punjab. Moreover, the Barnala government faced the crisis when the factional fight led to the split in the Akali Dal.

The militant violence continued to escalate much more seriously. Thereafter, the formation of a Panthic Committee and declaration of the armed struggle for Khalistan led to a mushroom growth of terrorist organizations and rising numbers of new recruits. In the 'Operation Black Thunder' in 1988, the Golden Temple was encircled by the police and militants were forced to surrender. However, soon after, violence escalated with increasing number of casualties.

Still another feature of the fourth phase is the social reform programme announced by the Panthic Committee led by Dr. Sohan Singh in 1987. This programme covered various dimensions of social practices and individual behaviour. For example, it was against the consumption of liquor and meat. Dowry was prohibited and the size of the *barat* (marriage party) was fixed on 11 persons. This was the first time that the militant movement intervened in the social life of the Sikh community.

In the fifth phase we find a series of initiatives undertaken at the national level by three successive Prime Ministers of which two were from the non-Congress political parties. When V.P. Singh took over as the Prime Minster in 1989, he appealed to the terrorists to join the mainstream. Chandra Shekhar, the successor of V.P. Singh as Prime Minister pursued the line of conciliation towards the militants through middlemen and direct negotiations. However, the killings in Punjab reached new heights and the police was thoroughly demoralized. There is, however, a reasonable basis to suggest that during the period when Chandra Shekhar was the Prime Minister the proportion of the militants among the killed began rising (Puri, Judge and Sekhon, 1999). In 1991, P.V. Narsimha Rao became the Prime Minister. When he decided to hold elections in Punjab in February 1992, the militant movement had already started the downward slide.

The sixth phase began when Beant Singh became the Chief Minister in 1992 following an election that saw a very effective boycott led by various Akali Dals and militant groups. The police were given extraordinary powers. Within a span of one year the back of terrorism was effectively broken. Barring a few incidents, the terrorist activities progressively declined to the extent of extinction by the end of 1993. One of the major events after its virtual suppression was the assassination of Beant Singh in 1995 by a suicide bomber.

III
Reasons for Joining the Movements

It is evident from the above discussion that in Punjab the Khalistan movement was larger in magnitude in terms of time, space, intensity and extensity than the Naxalite movement. It would be worthwhile to examine the participants of these two movements in terms of their caste background and reasons for joining the movements. It is generally assumed that since one of the movements was ideologically religious all the participants were from the same religious community. In the case of the Khalistan movement this was not the case. If exception proves the rule, then, we may say that though there were few Hindus in the movement, it was the movement of the Sikhs. The Naxalite movement was though a value-oriented movement, yet it was based on the secular ideology of creating a classless society. It is therefore expected that the participants in this movement could be drawn from any religious community. Thus, we have chosen the caste background of the participants of both the movements. It may be pointed out that in the context of the Indian society the caste is the key to the understanding of the social background of the individuals. The caste background of the individuals also provides an insight into their general socio-economic status due to a degree of correspondence between the caste and occupation.

We may now turn to the caste background of some of the participants in both the movements.[4] It is evident from the Table 1 that in both the movements an overwhelming proportion of the participants belonged to the Jat Sikh caste. Interestingly, the percentage of Jats in the Naxalite movement is higher than that of the Khalistan movement. Who are these Jats? The Jats are peasant proprietors of Punjab. They converted to Sikhism at the time of the fifth Guru of the Sikhs, Guru Arjan Dev. According to Irfan Habib (1976), there was a lag between the social status, which was low, and their economic achievement, which was high. The Sikh movement provided them the opportunity to raise their status. The Jats have remained a highly mobile caste among the Sikhs. Most of the Punjabis, who have migrated to the western countries, belong to this caste. Over the years, the Jats have experienced a tremendous change as a caste group. It has become heterogeneous from within as classes have emerged among them. It was found that in the case of the Naxalite movement most of these Jats belonged to the middle class, whereas in the case of the Khalistan movement the Jat participants belonged to lower middle classes (Puri, Judge and Sekhon, 1999; Judge, 2000). The proportion of the lower castes and classes in these movements presents an interesting case.

Table 1

Caste and Religious Background of the Participants in the Movements

*Caste Background**	*Naxalite Movement ***	*Khalistan Movement***
Jat (Sikh)	64 (81.00)	65 (76.47)
Brahmin/Khatri/Banya (Hindu)	06 (7.59)	—
Saini (Sikh)	01 (1.27)	—
Chhimba (Sikh)	01 (1.27)	
Tarkhan (Sikh)	01 (1.27)	—
Jheer (Sikh)	—	01 (1.18)
Bhatra (Sikh)	—	1 (1.18)
Nai (Sikh)	—	04 (4.71)
Ad-Dharmi (Hindu)	05 (6.33)	03 (3.52)
Mazbi (Sikh)	—	11 (12.94)
Muslim	01 (1.27)	—
Total	79 (100)	85 (100)

* Shows the religious background of the participants in brackets.

** Show percentages in brackets.

Note: It may be noted that since the samples are of unequal size, comparing the percentages makes the analysis.

In comparison with the Naxalite movement the proportion of the Dalit castes in the Khalistan movement was high. Most of the Dalits in the rural areas of Punjab belong to the class of agricultural labour. They are expected to be in larger number in the Naxalite movement than the Khalistan movement. The data indicate something, which is contrary to the assumption. One may argue that for the working class in Punjab religion has stronger appeal than the ideology of classlessness. However, there could be many reasons for this kind of discrepancy. The most important being the way the Naxalite movement operated during the phase of the implementation of the line of annihilation of the class enemies. The 'declassed' middle class revolutionary had to approach the working class members to know who should be annihilated. In Punjab, many respondents admitted that they did not approach the Dalits for shelter; rather they preferred their friend and middle class sympathizers (Judge, 1992). Conversely, the Khalistan movement welcomed any Sikh to join it. Its duration of one and half decades and its magnitude drew a considerable number of Mazhabis who belong to the scheduled castes.

Still another notable dimension of both the movements is the participation of the upper castes. In the Naxalite movement we find that 7.59 per cent of the Naxalites belonged to the upper castes such as Brahmin, Khatri or Banya, whereas no participant belonging to these castes was found in the villages studied.[5] One of the reasons for the absence of the upper castes is that most of them are Hindus and it is unlikely that they would participate in the movement from which they are ideologically excluded. However, there are upper caste Sikhs too. It may be added that most of the upper caste Sikhs are traders by occupation and they live in urban areas. There was only one village, namely, Mattewal, in which there was a substantial population of the Aroras. In this village, out of the total seven participants in the Khalistan movement, six belonged to the Jat caste, whereas one was Mazhabi. In the case of the trading castes the ideology of the Naxalite movement was antithetical, particularly for those who were traders, which might explain their less participation, but the Khalistan movement did not present such a case for the trading castes. It is therefore essential to look at the non-participation of the Khatris and Aroras in the Khalistan movement.

It may be pointed out at the outset that the trading is an occupation for which disturbances and violence are undesirable processes as these adversely affect the business and trade. Existentially, we may understand that the individuals involved in trading would develop a consciousness that perceives disturbances as wrong and thus should be avoided. As a routinized social reality, such a consciousness becomes a part of the cultural life of the occupational group. Conversely, it may be argued that if it is in the business interests of the traders to encourage violence and disturbances, then, they may go for it. In Mattewal, the Aroras encouraged terrorism in the village to force the migration of Hindu traders and they succeeded. However, these two aspects pass each other by and may co-exist. Still another argument could be that of the total Sikh population a majority of the Sikhs belong to the Jat caste. The Jats have been dominating in the Sikh affairs whether religious or political independence. The Khatri and Arora Sikhs have been marginalized as a result of which they have become indifferent to the Sikh issues. It seems that the absence or very little presence of the Khatris and Aroras in the Khalistan movement cannot be explained by one factor. The participation of the Jats and Mazhabis in the movement in a big way tends to suggest that it was a rural phenomenon and the upper caste Sikhs are predominantly urban. The movement, however, was not ideologically limited to the rural areas as had been the case with the Naxalite movement. The little response of the Khatris and Aroras may become clearer after the discussion of reasons for joining the movement.

It has become clear that the response of various caste groups to both the movements was not uniform. The Jats dominated the movements in spite of the radical differences in their ideologies. Before we discuss the reasons for joining the movement, a few remarks on the issue of the nature of data are required. It may be stated at the outset that giving the reasons, intentions and motivation of the individuals can always be questioned. An action is understood the way the actor attributes his meanings to it. The observer's attribution of meanings to the action may be different if not conflicting, from the way the actor had understood his meanings. The phenomenological perspective distinguishes two kinds of motives of action, namely, 'because' and 'in-order-to' motives. Though there is a reasonable uncertainty in the identification of reasons for joining the movement, yet it may be reminded that most of the actions are uniform as result of custom and usage or the inter-subjective nature of the social world. Since the actors can change their meanings they have attributed to the action, it is important that methodologically no single way of identification can provide the complete picture. In other words, the data on the reasons for joining the movement are qualitative in nature and cannot be easily verified. However, a reasonable estimation is always possible, particularly when the researcher is aware of various existential and social conditions of the selected participants. In the present case, the information regarding the reasons for joining has been largely gathered from the people who know the participants. These included the village people to which the participants belonged, the friends and relatives, and sometimes the participants themselves. In both the movements, many of the participants had died in encounters with the police and security forces and thus it was impossible to depend on one way of getting the information. The reasons for joining each movement have been shown in Table 2.

Table 2

Reasons for Joining the Movement

Reasons	*Naxalite Movement*	*Khalistan Movement*
Ideological Conviction	70 (88.60)	24 (28.24)
Influence of Sikh History	06 (7.59)	—
Police Harassment	01 (1.27)	03 (3.53)
Interfamily/Interpersonal Feuds	—	07 (8.24)
Personal Reasons other than feuds	01 (1.27)	08 (9.41)
To Make Money	—	03 (3.53)
Militant Appeal/*Shaukia*	01 (1.27)	40 (47.05)
Total	79 (100)	85 (100)

Note: Figures in brackets show percentages.

It is interesting to note that 88.60 per cent of the participants in the Naxalite movement joined due to ideological reasons, whereas only 28.24 per cent joined the Khalistan movement for these reasons. It has been already pointed out that the Maoist elements in the CPI-M left the party after the Naxalbari events took place and organized themselves as a separate party. Thus, most of the Naxalites were communists before the beginning of the movement. Another major source of the movement was the Punjab Students' Union—a student wing of the CPI-M. After the Naxalbari event the entire Union joined the Naxalites. On the other hand, the Khalistan movement was based on the religious ideology where the cadre was presumed to be available. The appeal of Sikhism remained limited and other factors began to dominate. How did it happen? The next part of the paper describes and analyzes the non-ideological reasons for joining the movements.

IV
Making Sense of Non-ideological Reasons

This last part of the paper, as pointed out earlier, focuses mainly on the issue of non-ideological reasons for joining the terrorist movements. It is evident from Table 2 that in the case of the Naxalite movement 7.59 per cent of the participants joined it as they were influenced by the Sikh history. The researcher interviewed four of them and they were asked to explain this reason in details. Their argument was that after reading the stories of great sacrifices made by the Sikh Gurus they also wanted to emulate their life achievements. The communist movement was the only one that seemed near to the ideals of the Sikh history. However, after they joined, they realized the difference and as they were serious readers of history and literature they found no problem in accepting the ideology. Later, the Naxalite movement began and they found the most appropriate moment to put their thoughts into action.

In the case of the Khalistan movement, the non-ideological reasons dominated for providing the motives to the participants to join it. Before we explain why nearly half (47.05%) of the participants joined due to the militant appeal of the movement, it is appropriate to take stock of reasons, such as feuds and other personal reasons. Feuds in Punjabi society are linked with what Bourdieu (1970) calls 'honour and shame' in the case of Kabyles of Algeria. Vengeance for maintaining the honour of the family is must, otherwise the family would be put to shame for its failure of its members. Such situations emerge when serious offences, like murder of the family member or forcible occupation of land, are made. As most of the Jats joined the movement, the nature and content of vengeance largely revolved round land. Pettigrew (1978) has convincingly shown the nature and extent of the feuds that surpass the boundaries of the fighting families and extend to the state politics. Within the structure of inter-family feuds the reasons for joining the movement could vary from one to the other person. In the case of Khalistan movement, some of the reasons were as follows: a particular family had murdered the close kin, a member of the family of enemies has joined the terrorist movement, dispute over property with the other family, and the opponent might have insulted the member of the family.

In addition to the feuds, certain personal circumstances led the young boys to join the militant movement. In most of these cases, a friend or a relative who had joined the movement became the reason for joining it. One simple reason was that he could inspire them to join. The other reason was that some incidence of murder in the village compelled them to join the movement as they anticipated the police harassment due to their connections with the militants.

All these non-ideological reasons discussed so far were limited in their extensity and magnitude. The most important reason was the militant appeal, particularly in the case of the Khalistan movement. At the time of data collection, the researcher was struck by word *shaukia* the people used to explain this reason. It literally means "for the fun of it". To make sense of this expression at the level of meanings, it may be stated that 47.05 per cent of the militants joined the movement "for the fun of it". Such an observation seems unbelievable, as most of us are in the habit of getting convinced, particularly in the case of extreme situations that there cannot be some unrelated factor underlying such circumstances. Without losing objectivity the researcher is expected to understand such ostensibly unrelated expressions. The proceeding discussion is aimed at the explication of this reason for joining the Khalistan movement.

Joining a militant movement is a serious act, in the sense that the participant is also putting his own life in danger. Though the Punjabi poetry and literature is full of stories of and praises for the Sikhs (sometimes Punjabis) willingly sacrificing their lives, yet such stories tend to organically link the sacrifice with the cause or ideology. In cultural terms, as pointed out by Nahar Singh (1999), the Punjabi folklore puts tremendous emphasis on death and consumerism. The central motif is that since the ultimate reality is death, one should enjoy the life.[6] This is not confined to the folklore; it also reflects in the living style of the Punjabis. However, the recent shift of Punjabis from stoicism to Epicureanism is related with the green revolution in Punjab. To a great extent, the conflicting consequences of green revolution have a lot to do with the Khalistan movement. The green revolution was a phenomenon of high agricultural growth rate in Punjab. It began in the late sixties as a result of the introduction of hybrid seeds and chemical fertilizers, provision of institutional credit, promotion of irrigation projects and development of link roads in the villages. The Indian government sponsored all this and the Punjabi farmers accepted this change that ushered in a new era in the state.

The green revolution phenomenon gave tremendous prosperity to the middle and big farmers of Punjab. There was an increase in both the intensity and extensity of the cropping pattern. Above all, it created wheat-rice monoculture, which was market-oriented agrarian production system. The new technology was labour intensive. The crops required irrigation, chemical fertilizers and pesticides for high productivity. Since the number of crops increased to more than two, the pressure on the farmer to complete the harvesting operation within the limited time increased. Thus, the migrant labour from other states of India fulfilled the demand for labour in Punjab. As the green revolution progressed, more and more labour reached Punjab. The farmer of Punjab, who was predominantly a middle peasant, changed his role from 'owner cultivator' to the 'owner supervisor'. As the family labour became free from the farming, it withdrew from the labour market rather than shifting to non-agricultural sector. In such a situation, as pointed out by Gill and Singhal (1984), the sub-division of land due to inheritance emerged as an important factor. The middle farmer's sons could not retain the status of their father, because the size of holdings each of them would inherit could not be sufficient to sustain his middle peasant status.

It is evident from the above discussion that the green revolution created two-fold consequences in Punjab. First, the migrant labour made the peasant free from expending his own labour in the agrarian production. Secondly, over a period of time, the sub-division of landholdings threatened the peasantry, because the benefits could not reach the next generation. The marginalization of holdings could be handled had they joined the white-collar occupations for which the formal education was indispensable. In this situation, the symbolic universe of the Jat peasants shaped their response. They avoided becoming manual labourers, as the wage work is regarded as of lower status. The lack of formal education closed the avenues for them to seek employment in the cities. Thus, a class of idle youth emerged in the rural areas of Punjab. This was particularly more pronounced in the Amritsar and Gurdaspur districts. This youth was available for the recruitment to the Khalistan movement, but it required an incentive to join the movement, which was provided by the Prime Minister of India in 1989.

V.P. Singh became the Prime Minister in 1989 and in his first speech to the nation he mentioned the Punjab problem wherein he said that there was a need to give a healing touch to the hurt feelings of the Sikhs and bring the youth into the mainstream. The process of bringing the insurgent groups into the mainstream was not a new phenomenon in India. At that time, the recent example was that of Assam where the Assam Gana Parishad (AGP) came to power as a result of long-drawn movement that ended when the leaders signed an accord with the then Prime Minister, Rajiv Gandhi. The leaders of the movement were now running the government in Assam. In the backdrop of such an occurrence, it seemed natural that the police force in Punjab faced a dilemma. The militants could be their ministers. There is a reasonable basis to argue that during 1989-90, when V.P. Singh was the Prime Minister, the police actions against the militants in Punjab declined (Puri, Judge and Sekhon, 1999) Simultaneously, the youth in villages made idle by the green revolution saw it as an opportunity to make hay while the sun was shining. They saw militancy as an avenue to economic and possibly political gains. Already, the Surjit Singh Barnala government provided jobs to those who had participated in the 'Dharam Yudh Morcha'. The momentary inactivity of the police and the orientation of the youth led to their joining the terrorist movement.

To understand why people identified *shaukia* as the reason for joining the Khalistan movement, we must not regard it in the lighter vein. Behind this reason is located the entire cultural milieu of Punjab. In the existential sense it may be argued that this idle youth had lost meanings in life. It may be asked how did this loss of meanings occur? In one sense it has a lot to do with the way the post-independent India developed its democratic and civil society institutions. The recognition of diversity paved the way for a strong centre, the objective of which was to create a powerful intervening force in the situation of clash of diverse identities and aspirations. This vision did not prevent the process of politicization of these identities such as caste, region, religion etc. At the same time, the economic policies and progress failed to deliver what the leaders of independent India promised. We have still not tried to analyze what would have happened had the land reform laws been fully implemented. The green revolution in Punjab did not only bring prosperity, but also raised the aspirations for a radiant future. This radiant future soon became an illusion for the peasants as the simple demographic factor of sub-division of landholdings worked to nullify the gains of high agricultural production. At this juncture, there was no alternative to choose and marginalization of peasantry started occurring. In such an economic scenario one of the paths they chose had its origin in the symbolic universe of the Sikhs. The tradition of martyrdom in the Sikh history which, as pointed out by Fenech (2000), was constructed during the Singh Sabha movement in the late nineteenth century, became the basis for providing meanings. In this sense, it was not simply a process of loss of meanings, but also a search for new meaning, irrespective of whether it is normatively justified.

There is no doubt that in joining the movement without ideological reasons a degree of adventure is involved and the actor is aware of the dangers involved in terrorist acts. The perception of the people in characterizing such joining of the movement as *shaukia* does also need some attention. In that sense existential conditions play the decisive role in motivating the actors to join the movement. People's view of the Khalistan movement was that since it was the movement of the Khalsa, anybody who joined it must be religious devout. They found that the youth of their own village were joining the movement without any such religious conviction. As a result, they used the expression *shaukia* to explain such cases. It is also the character of the Khalistan movement that made it possible for a large number of young people to join it. Anybody who was a Sikh could be a potential recruit to the movement. Thus, any Sikh could verbally show his allegiance to the cause of the Sikhs and the Khalistan and join the movement. The process of recruitment and the non-ideological considerations were the main reasons for a large number of young boys joining the Khalistan movement.

V
Conclusion

Two militant movements were examined to understand why the individuals join violent movements. These two movements, namely, the Naxalite movement and the Khalistan movement, had distinct, if not conflicting, ideologies. Ideologically, limited individuals could join the Naxalite movement, as it was a communist movement aimed at transforming the society through insurrection. It adopted violent methods to achieve its goal. On the contrary, the Khalistan movement tended to assume all Sikhs as the potential recruits, as all the Sikhs could join it. In spite of these ideological distinctions of fundamental nature, both the movements actually recruited the peasant proprietary caste of the Jat Sikhs. However, the proportion of the participants joining the Khalistan movement, due to non-ideological reasons, was considerably higher than that of the Naxalite movement. It however may not be deduced that the Naxalite movement did not attract the youth, which was not committed to its ideology. As the foregoing analysis shows, there were participants in the movement due to non-ideological reasons. To end the discussion, it may be argued that it is not necessary that people join a militant movement due to their ideological convictions. Socio-economic and existential conditions are primary in giving the platform, but the cultural conditions become the springboard for providing the orientation, motivation and intention to the people to join movements that entail an ideology of violent means.

Notes

1. The movements based on the notion of the arrival of the prophet or the Guru are called messianic movements. Messianic movements may also turn violent, but it depends on the claims of the leaders. Fuchs (1965) has studied messianic movements in India.
2. It may be pointed out that the concept of terrorism has undergone changes over a period of time. At one point of time terrorism was treated as a stage in the revolutionary or national liberation struggle. It was generally regarded as the weapon of the week. Trotsky made a distinction between 'red terror' and 'white terror'. He regarded the former as positive and liberating, whereas, for him, the latter was oppressive. However, presently the notion of terrorism has become normative. It implies that there cannot be any analytical distinction on any criterion to characterize it as desirable or undesirable. We may now comment that with the changed world order after the collapse of Soviet Union, the use of collective violence to achieve even objectives like freedom, social change, etc. is undesirable. As a result, the use of the world 'terrorism' has been avoided in this paper. Instead, we have used the expression 'terrorist methods' not only to avoid the present normative characterisation of terrorism, but also to make it implicit in the use of expression that it was a conscious choice of the leaders of the movement.
3. Most of the discussion on the Khalistan movement is based on the following works: Akbar (1985), Harminder Kaur (1990) and Narayanan (1996).
4. It may be informed that the data for these tables have been collected through field-work by using the interview method. However, in the case of the Naxalite movement the information was gathered by personal interviews of the Naxalites as well as by interviewing others who knew them. In the latter case, 'others' meant friends, co-participants and village fellows. In the case of the Khalistan movement the information was collected from the village people through interviews. It may be added that one of the major problems faced by the researchers in the study of the violent movements after

their suppression is the difficulty in finding out the participants. In the case of the Khalistan movement most of the militants had been killed in clash with the police and para-military forces.

5. As the total number of the participants in each of the movements is not of the same, the analysis of the data has only been done by comparing the percentages.
6. A couplet from famous folk song that expresses the death as ultimate reality is as follows:
   Do din khed lei, maujan mann lai,
   Tain bhaj javana kangana kach dia.

   (Play and enjoy for a couple of days, Oh! bangle made up of glass you will break).

   Such folk songs are in abundance and, according to Nahar Singh, provide the Punjabis an impetus towards consumerism. Simultaneously, these also push some to perform heroic deeds.

References

Akbar, M.J. 1985. *India: The Siege Within.* New York: Viking Penguin.

Banerjee, Sumanta. 1980. *In the Wake of Naxalbari: A History of the Naxalite Movement in India.* Calcutta: Subarnarekha.

Blumer, Herbert. 1957. 'Collective Behavior' in J.B. Gittler (ed.), *Review of Sociology: Analysis of Decade.* New York: John Wiley & Sons.

Bourdieu, Pierre. 1970. *Algeria 1960.* Cambridge: Cambridge University Press.

Dasgupta, Biplab. 1974. *The Naxalite Movement.* Calcutta: Allied Publishers.

Fenech, Louis E. 2000. *Martyrdom in Sikh Tradition: Playing the Game of Love.* New Delhi: Oxford University Press.

Fuchs, Stephen. 1965. *Rebellious Prophets: A Study of Messianic Movements in Indian Religion.* Bombay: Asia Publishing House.

Gill, Sucha Singh and K.C. Singhal. 1984. 'Genesis of Punjab Problem: Its Historical Roots', *Economic and Political Weekly*, April 7.

Habib, Irfan. 1976. 'Jats of Punjab and Sind', in Harbans Singh and N.G. Barrier (eds.), *Punjab Past and Present: Essays in Honour of Dr. Ganda Singh.* Patiala: Punjabi University, pp. 92-103.

Hebrele, Rudolf. 1949. 'Observations on the sociology of social movements', *American Sociological Review*, 14.

Judge, Paramjit S. 1992. *Insurrection to Agitation: The Naxalite Movement in Punjab.* Bombay: Popular Prakashan.

—. 2000. 'The Naxalite movement in Punjab' in Harish K. Puri and Paramjit S. Judge (eds.), *Social and Political Movements: Readings on Punjab.* Jaipur: Rawat.

Kaur, Harminder. 1990. *Blue Star over Amritsar*. New Delhi: Ajanta.

Narayanan, V.N. 1996. *Tryst with Terror: Punjab's Turbulent Decade.* New Delhi: Ajanta.

Pettigrew, Joyce. 1978. *Robber Noblemen: A Study of Political System of the Sikh Jats.* New Delhi: Ambika Publications.

Puri, Harish K., Paramjit S. Judge and Jagrup S. Sekhon. 1999. *Terrorism in Punjab: Understanding Grassroots Reality.* New Delhi: Har-Anand Publications.

Puri, Harish K. and Paramjit S. Judge. 2000. 'Khalistan movement' in Puri Harish K. and Paramjit S. Judge (eds.), *Social and Political Movements: Readings on Punjab.* Jaipur: Rawat.

Rao, M.S.A. 1978. 'Introduction', in M.S. Rao (ed.), *Social Movements in India,* Vol. I. New Delhi: Manohar.

Russell, Charles A. and Bowman, H. Miller. 1985. 'Profile of a terrorist', in Freedman, Lawrence and Alexander Yonah (eds.), *Perspectives on Terrorism.* New Delhi: IIPC.

Singh, Nahar. 1999. 'Punjab da virsa: Lokdharai paripekh' (Punjabi). Paper presented in the Third Annual Convention of NRI Sabha, Jalandhar.

Smelser, Neil J. 1961. *Theory of Collective Behavior.* London: Routledge & Kegan Paul.

Steinhoff, Patricia G. 1976. 'The portrait of a terrorist', *Asian Survey* XVI: 9, September.

Thorton, Thomas P. 1964. 'Terror as a weapon of political agitation', in Eckstein, H. (ed.), *Internal War*. New York: Free Press, pp. 71-99.

Wilkinson, Paul. 1977. *Terrorism and the Liberal State.* London: Macmillan.

7

Cultural Nationalism and Tensions in the North-East India

N. SUDHAKAR RAO

I

The paper aims to examine conflicts and tensions in the North-East India in the background of cultural nationalism that the early nationalists espoused. While not disregarding the significance of various explanations already offered for manifestation of these conflicts such as immigrations, competition for scare resources, ethnic identity maintenance and so on in Marxist and non-Marxist frameworks, the present paper focuses on nationalism—another important dimension. Nationalism has been one of the most powerful constructs, both for political ends and nation-building processes. It is essentially social in nature in that it bases on 'we'-'they' or 'self'-'other' dyadic premises. Aloysius (1997) distinguishes two varieties of nationalism in the making of India: cultural nationalism and political nationalism. The cultural nationalism, as developed by Ernest Gellner, combines culture and power based on traditional hierarchies. Taking clue from him, it is argued in this paper that the cultural nationalism, as certain dominant groups dearly cherish, continues to operate as a strong undercurrent of the overt political nationalism apparent in the Constitution of India.

According to Aloysius, from the beginning, the top hierarchy of the society constructed the nationalism so as to continue the old hierarchy that suffered serious threat by the colonisers. They had seen their religion, culture and interests in danger. He writes: "Nationalism in the sub-continent sought the transfer of power from the alien culture to preserve the prenation form of differential power realization within society; and herein lies the basically contradictory nature of Indian nationalism" (1997: 109). The contradictory nature lies between the pronounced political nationalism sharing of power on the basis modern values (equality and without linguistic and cultural prejudices) and the cultural nationalism that bases on the Sanskritic, *sanatan* Hindu traditions in pursuit of preserving the cultural heritage and maintenance of traditional social hierarchies. In the history of nationalism, socially dominant groups were not only able to muster the positions in bureaucracy and political machinery but also continued their socio-cultural dominance. Thus, the socio-economic change brought by the British did not bring any fundamental change in the social system. The nationalists had power at two levels: in secular organizations and religio-cultural organizations. Most members of the Indian National Congress were also members of different religio-cultural organizations such as the cow protection society, Hindu *sabhas*, Arya Samaj etc. Exceptions to this rule had been minimum. The Congress leaders could easily pass from one into the other without any sense of contradiction. In fact, "it is how the secularity and 'national'ness of the Indian nationalist movement in general, and of the Congress in particular, was maintained" (ibid: 14). This feature overshadowed the diverse religious, linguistic and ethnic groups and at the most the Congress sought cooperation of the groups and did not like these groups maintain separate identities. The ideology of cultural nationalism was articulated through newspapers, magazines and other media. However, Dalits, Shudras and Ati-Shudras and other communities were less willing to join hands on unequal terms as an ideal part of nationalism. But, they did consent to the political national ideology articulated through social egalitarianism and abolition of ascriptive privileges. They subscribed to democratization of society and extended series of rights to lower caste masses that facilitated joining the nationalist movement.

Mahatma Gandhi's entry changed features of the nationalist movement. He synthesized the cultural and political nationalisms with the blend of *varnashrama dharma*, cow protection, Khilafat and untouchability. However, the Gandhian rhetoric of moral reform, critique of western civilization and restitution of our own traditional ways of life, caused embitterment among Muslim masses and depressed classes. But, finally, he managed to persuade the latter to follow the immediate elite agenda of apparent anti-imperialism. The lower caste communities or minorities and ethnic groups could not flee from the oppression of upper castes or attempted sabotage but in fairness attempted to avail themselves of the new found opportunities in politics and economic spheres. However, the dominators continued to articulate ideology of political nationalism maintaining cultural domination over the marginal population skilfully avoiding fulfilment of the aspirations of the masses. Nationalism distanced slowly from the nation and moved towards formation of a state system, where the traditional domination was transferred into state power.

II

One nation theory and national integration *ipso facto* presupposes existence of multiple nations and groups to be brought under the umbrella of a nation and the need to integrate them. The former situation is perceived as threat to the very existence of the nationhood achieved by great struggle and payment of heavy price. It contains the dichotomies of mainstream-periphery, superordination-subordination, and giver-receiver and the fear of disintegration. It envisages strategies of homogenization, cultural or social domination, so as to bring 'they' into the fold of 'we' by coercion or persuasion. Since the one nation theory has taken the disposition of cultural nationalism, given the socio-cultural milieu of the North-East, eruption of several problems are expected in the North-East India. India, more particularly the North-East India, is multi-cultural. This cultural pluralism envelops the whole range of languages, dialects, religions, sects, food habits, dress, marriage practices and so on. Diversity in ways of life has been organized in a particular way which ensured that it was reproduced from generation to generation. It is also a fact that the diversity of Indian civilization is the result of orthogenetic as well as heterogenetic processes accommodating new elements from outside over the entire course of history without loosing its identity. It is both a source of strength and weakness. Thus, Andre Beteille (2001: 36) dismisses any fear of identity loss. It has to be noted that the multi-culturalism provides single identity to its citizens with modern, democratic and secular constitution based on three related institutions: (1) a secular state governed by the impersonal rule of law; (2) citizenship without regard for distinctions of caste, creed and gender; and (3) open and secular public institutions mediating between citizen and state. But, these institutions have not worked well as had been expected.

The nation-building process though started on these tenets, the cultural nationalism has continued to facilitate the building of a majority whose hegemony is still unchallenged. This process involved in minority persecution, ethnic cleansing, denial of political rights to smaller groups and atrocities due to which exodus of the persecuted is taking place. Interestingly, this process then accelerated and emerged as a pattern because the minorities also constructed a national identity and strived to build a majority for themselves (c.f. Nag, 2001: 4759). The nationhood, in this background, we may note as Nag points out "the search for nationhood in the subcontinent always focussed ethnicity, culture and religion" (ibid: 4760) contradicts the constitutional framework. Similarly, Oommen observes, "the central issues of nation building in India revolve around the persistent tension between the Hindi-speaking twice born Hindus, who define themselves as the norm-setters and value-givers, the cultural mainstream, and a multiplicity of other primordial collectivities occupying the periphery of the system, depending upon their positioning in the socio-cultural space of India" (1993: 473).

III

With this background we shall examine the situation in the North-East, particularly Assam. The history of nationalism in Assam is no way different from others. During the pre-independence period, the hill people were never under the rule and subjugation of the plains people or Rajahs of Ahom. In fact, very often, the hill people used to plunder the villages in plains, harvested the crops of the villages stealthily and took away their cattle. Thus, these two communities constantly engaged themselves in fights and feuds due to plunder and control over resources. The chieftains and Rajahs used to reconciliate the offenders and victims, and at times displayed force to bring peace between the communities. The local communities felt the entry of the British into the region and interference in the affairs of the local communities unnecessary, but it was unavoidable, and the presence of the British changed the entire social and political scenario of the region. The British interfered in the local politics of the chieftains, tactfully established their supremacy and ultimately became the rulers. In their administration, they followed the policy of autonomy to the tribals and isolationist approach. However, absolute peace did not exist between the British and the hill people. There were incidences of upsurge at different times and these were demonstrations of resistance to the domination of British. The tribals did not participate in the freedom struggle, nor did they entertain the idea of tribal solidarity in the region or national freedom. In this regard, we may note Mazumdar's reference to Thomas and Taylor (1965: 93): "We were not so fully involved in the national struggle for freedom as to enthuse us with the idea of a common national destiny, so that many tribes were not fully aware of the meaning of independence for themselves or the nation at large. Even some who were aware of it continued to feel themselves to be neglected people" (1993: 272).

The story of freedom struggle very briefly is as follows: Under the guidance of Maniram Dewan and Pioli Barua and Ahom king Kandarpeswar Singh, Assam rose to the occasion of insurgency—Sepoy Mutiny. Assam leaders protested the Rowlatt Bills and Jullianwala Bagh massacre by organizing several public meetings. Similarly, Assam observed 25 October 1919 as the Khilafat Day by burying the differences between Hindus and Muslims under the influence of Mahatma Gandhi. Assam Association of National Congress led the non-coöperation movement under the leadership of Nabin Chandra Bardoloi. Mahatma Gandhi's visit to Assam in August 1921 had a galvanizing impact on Assam in organizing the protest rallies. With several twists and turns in the course of independence, Assam reached to the point of gaining separate identity by dissociating itself with Bengal in 1946 under the leadership of Gopinath Bardoloi.

It was the middle class or petty bourgeoisie—educated elites, lawyers, teachers and so on—that actively participated in the freedom struggle. This class came to existence mainly due the socio-economic changes brought about by the colonial government. These freedom fighters formed Assam Association of the Congress Party, and they had roots in the rural areas being Mauzdars (revenue collectors) and members of *satra* (religious institution of Vaisnava sect). They, thus, strongly espoused the cultural nationalism as an ideology of middle class. The Assamese society in general accepted the middle class and its own values, and there was a kind of general consent by the subordinate classes to the domination of the middle class. This consent was acquired through co-option of the subordinate classes. Sharma (1990: 139-40) states that this sort of domination led to several problems in the development of Assamese society.

The Assamese cultural nationalism sprang up with the demand of replacement of Bengali with Assamese as court language and with the referendum of Sylhet district of Assam following demarcation line of the Muslim and the non-Muslim majority areas of Assam at the time of independence. The ascended middle class was insensitive to the issues of the ethnic minorities in the late nineteenth and early twentieth centuries. This had led to resentment on the domination of this middle class and formation of organizations like Tribal League. However, the elites of these communities were not in a position to seriously challenge the Assamese (Baruah, 1994: 269-70; Bokth, 2000). Assimilation of these ethnic groups was sought more rigorously by making Assamese as official language.

The passion for linguistic state rose to greater height after 1947 when the middle class Assamese availed themselves most of the opportunities provided by independence. Later, the language policy of Assam, Assamese as compulsory subject in the schools, prerequisite for employment and Assamese to be official language, caused widespread resistance from the tribal people who speak different languages and dialects as well as Bengalis in Assam. Strong resistance came from the Bengalis of Barak valley resulting in violence and deaths.

The transfer of power to the middle class Assamese leaders after independence meant to the tribal people loss of autonomy, imposition of tribal and non-tribal hierarchies and cultural domination. Baruah's observation is worth noting here: "All small nationalities viewed the intolerant and expansionist tendencies of Indian nationalism of the Hindi-Hindu-Brahmanical variety as a threat to their cultural identity" (1994: 247). The nation-building process was viewed as legitimization of authority over the peripheral areas. Use of force for rule compliance was seen as domination. Necessarily, it had led to immigration of non-tribals for administration of the state or trade and business purposes from the plains resulting in the formation of heterogenous population, urbanization, and appearance of alien religions and floating of new ideas which are seen as cultural domination imposed on the natives leading to de-tribalization.

The domination of high-caste Assamese in Assam has been clearly pointed out by Monirul Hussain. He writes that the tribal minorities "remained socially, culturally, economically and politically exploited and the most oppressed group together with the non-autochthnous tribals of Assam's tea plantations and the Na-Asamiya Muslims—a predominantly peasant community. The official imposition of Asamiya language backed by powerful social movements led by the Assamese bourgeoisie made the tribals suspicious about the motives of the relatively advanced high castes" (1994: 291-92).

The plain tribes of Assam had not been sailing with the dominant non-tribal community in the freedom movement. The issues that troubled the plain tribes were: (1) establishment of their distinct ethnic identity; (2) participation in the political affairs of the state; (3) appointment in government jobs; and (4) lack of adequate facilities of modern system of education (Choudhury, 1989: 107). In this way, as the tribals were disgruntled, the Assam Congress expressed very eagerness to win the cooperation of tribals, its leaders were however never really sympathetic to the cause of tribals as Choudhury notes (ibid: 110). The demand of the tribals for scheduled areas or autonomy in the plains did not materialize. When the euphoria of sovereign state ended, due to encroachment of tribal lands by non-tribals and domination of Assamese language and culture, the problem surfaced again by the initiative of Bodos with the formation of Bodo Sahitya Sabha in 1952. The problem became acute since 1967 and continues till today. The hill tribes, such as Khasi, Garo, Mizo, Cachari, Mikir and so on, felt sense of deprivation as also being treated as second class citizens. In this case, Nair quotes Hiren Gohain: "During the previous decades, the Centre had silently delegated to the largely caste-Hindu Assamese elite the role of the gendarme in the North-East. The Assamese ruling class had always played that role with gusto, to the point of wielding the *danda* on the aspiration of all the weaker nationalities of the region" (1989: 51). Thus, in the nation-building process of Assam, a large majority of the tribes have not participated and there has not been equity in sharing of power.

Dissatisfied with the administration of Assam state, which remained largely with the non-tribals, development and language policy and cultural domination, the tribes of Naga, Mizo, Khasi and Jaintia hills demanded statehood which was granted at different times. The tribal people were apprehensive of the domination of immigrant plainsmen. "Even some of their leaders felt that India should recognize them not as their subordinate part but as friends with sovereign power in their internal matters within their territories" (Hussain, 1989: 140). The struggles for statehood and boundary disputes were matters of conflict.

The Assam movement that targeted the foreigners turned out to be communal in its content and the Asom Gana Parishad (AGP) that captured power through this movement in the state gradually disowned the Muslims who supported the party to come to power (Srikanth, 1999). In order to prevent infiltration of foreigners, the Assam government introduced the

Prevention of Infiltration from Pakistan (PIP) scheme to detect and deport such infiltrators. But, this seems to have resulted in the repression of the Na-Asamiya Muslims who migrated from East Bengal much before the partition and were Asamiyaized. Hussain writes: "The operation of PIP scheme terrorised the virtually unorganised and defenseless rural Muslim peasantry—particularly the Na-Asamiya Muslims throughout the Brahmaputra Valley" (2000: 4519). Thus, the caste Hindu population of Assam could not see the Muslim citizens as equal partakers of the fruits of independence.

IV

It is now necessary to examine the role of Bharatiya Janata Party (BJP) in Assam in the present context because the cultural nationalism described above, of late, has emerged very forcefully in the ideology of *Hindutva.* The BJP has adopted *Hindutva* as a political ideology within the framework of "one nation, one people and one culture". Dubbed as communal party, the BJP is held responsible for incitation of communal passions and tensions in the country with its associate cultural organizations like RSS, VHP etc. Even though, a large number of Muslims and Christians are inhabiting in the region and carrying out missionary activities, the BJP had no role to play till 1991. But, since then, it showed its presence in a moderate way by capturing two seats in the parliament in the last two elections. It could poll votes from 25 to 30 per cent and thus emerged as main rival of Congress party in 1999 parliamentary elections (Srikanth, 1999: 3414). In the assembly elections, it bagged 10 seats in 1991, five in 1996 and eight in 2001.

Assamese identity crisis even prior to independence as mentioned before and its escalation after independence hampered the growth of the BJP in Assam. The cultural nationalism of BJP kind seems to have originated in the formation of Assam Provincial Hindu Sabha. In its session on 27 November 1941 presided over by Veer Savarkar, the Hindu Sabha resolved to resist the attempts made by the then Muslim League government in Assam to keep Assam as a part of Pakistan (Nag, 1990: 147). During this period of turmoil, communal tensions and riots continued till the formation of Pakistan. In the post-independence period, the communal tensions though ebbed out considerably, the problem of foreigners' immigration into Assam kept the Assamese on tenterhooks. In spite of keeping the Bengalis at bay by achieving Assam state, the Assamese caste Hindus, along with the Na-Asamiyas, were concerned with the domination of Bengalis in the state. Hence, the Assam movement sprang up in a big way against the Bengalis. In the given circumstances, the BJP was helpless to separate Hindus and Muslims but perhaps was waiting for an opportunity. When the National Democratic Alliance (NDA) came to power at the Centre, the wave of BJP spread over Assam also that enabled the party to bag 10 assembly seats in 1991 as maiden innings. With this victory, the BJP became an important political party, and later it tried to maintain political alliance with the ruling AGP, of course, there was no absolute support of all members of the party to this alliance.

As stated above, the Muslim (Na-Asamiya) voters did support the AGP, which was dominated by middle class caste Hindu Assamese in the beginning and worked together for Assamese identity and control of Bengali domination. However, friction between the caste Hindu Assamese and Muslims began with the emergence of United Liberation Front of Assam (ULFA), the extremist insurgent group that has been critical of the AGP government for not dealing properly with the foreigners' issue. The AGP also was unhappy with the ISI's purported support to ULFA. In fact, the caste Hindu Assamese began to suspect the Muslim's support to ISI when the news reports flashed cracking down of ISI network in Assam. Fuel was added to this when Lt. General S.K. Sinha, Governor of Assam submitted his report to the central government in 1998 about large-scale illegal infiltration of Muslims into Assam posing grave threat to the security of the country. This situation became handy for the BJP to reiterate its stand against the Muslims, and the disillusioned Assamese caste Hindus now inclined towards the BJP leaving AGP and Congress camps. Thus, the BJP which did not have any ground in upper Assam became victorious in Guwahati and Nagaon parliamentary constituencies in 1999 elections. Now, the polarization between the Hindus and Muslims in various places is obvious though the situation is not tense. It is very unlikely that a situation would arise as that of Gujarat since considerable number of Muslims are present in the state. In fact, 21 of the 125 MLAs are Muslims. However, the overall situation is not different from the rest of India.

V

The Hindu-Christian relations in the North-East have, by and large, been harmonious. It may be due to their substantial number and state's support in Mizoram, Nagaland and Meghalaya, but recent attacks on the Christian priests in Manipur put the region in the map of atrocities committed against the Christians along with Gujarat and Orissa. The concept of 'Hindu Rashtra' held by some cultural organizations and political parties, and accusations cast against the Christian missionaries and institutions by individuals, are indicative of religious intolerance in the state. The Christians of North-East are considered to be citizens at the periphery, not belonging to the mainstream, not only because of their religion being of outside origin but also because of the low social status epitomized in the category of 'tribals' the concept which is detested (see Imchen, 1993: 105; Pakem, 1993: 327). Even if there is no manifested communal disharmony between the Hindus and the Christians but certainly hatred is harboured by the majority of Hindus towards the minority Christians, which also forms a nerve centre of conflicts. Efforts of the Ramakrishna Mission and the Vanvasi Kalyan Ashram and several other organizations may be viewed as counter-actions against the Christians so as to either allow the tribals to practise their own religion or convert them to Hinduism. The Christian churches or missions have often been criticized by the majority of caste Hindus of the region as agents that are encouraging terrorist activities or secessionist ideas and even sowing seeds of anti-national sentiments.

VI

We find the working of the ideology of cultural nationalism of the dominant community among the tribals of the North-East also. Its hegemonic influence can be noticed among the minorities who are constructing national identity on the basis of ethnicity. The Bodo Sahitya Sabha, as a prominent cultural organization, contributed to the rise of Bodos, conscientizing people with ethnocentric ideas and rising militancy among them. The Bodo militants have attempted to cleanse the Bodoland massacring hundreds of Na-Asmiya Muslim peasants, Santhals and Nepalis to establish their supremacy as Bodoland for Bodos but not for others. Not only that, the Bodos claimed Koch Rajbangshis as belonging to the same racial stock as of Bodos in an effort of expansion and homogenization, but the latter vehemently refused the claim of Bodos. In the same way, Kacharis claimed Dimasa as their own, but the latter again rejected the claim (Baruah, 1994: 270-72). After the state formation, the Khasis in Meghalaya turned against Bengalis and other non-tribal immigrants (Thomas, 2000). In Mizoram, the Christian tribals are reported to have been up against the non-Christian tribes coercing them to accept Christianity as an effort to homogenize Mizoram with the Christian tribal population. More than 50,000 Reangs had to flee from Mizoram to Assam and Tripura due to violence (Chowdhury, 2002: 2-3; Nag, 2001: 47-57). Thus, cultural nationalism based on ethnicity, language and religion subverting the constitutional nationhood has become order of the day disregarding secularism, democracy and egalitarianism even by the minority groups. In these cases also, traditional dominant communities have assumed state power in the nation-state system.

VII

The above discussion suggests the presence and at times overt working of cultural nationalism in the North-East India. Aloysius' (1997) contention that the cultural nationalism taken over by the political nationalism and finally enshrined in the Constitution, has not brought in the nationhood, seems to be true more so in case of the North-East, especially in Assam. The cultural nationalism that overshadowed the nationalists covertly or overtly during the freedom struggle did not end with the independence. It got transformed into a paradigm of articulation between groups. Therefore, the ethnic groups and minorities in turn employed the same to define their national identity and formation of little nationhood. It is high time that the national leaders wake up to seriously ponder over the issues of nation-building elaborately and clearly spread over the pages of the Constitution of India. Finally, one may agree with Oommen who states: "India cannot built an authentic nation-state by building a cultural mainstream reducing the numerous collectivities of the periphery to status of marginals. We can only have a nation-state with multiple cultural 'centres' " (1993: 473).

References

Aloysius, G. 1997. *Nationalism Without a Nation in India.* New Delhi: Oxford University Press.

Baruah, A.K. 1994. "Middle Class Hegemony and the National Question in Assam", in Milton S. Sangma (ed.), *Essays on North-East India.* New Delhi: Indus Publishing Company, pp. 242-277.

Beteille, Andre. 2001. "Seeding the Topsoil", *Outlook,* Vol. XLI No. 32: 36.

Bokth, Humayun. 2000. "Emergence of the Bodo Movement: A Sociological Analysis". Paper presented at the National Seminar on "Development of STs and SCs in the North-East India in the New Millennium" organized by the Department of Sociology, Assam University, Silchar, December 8-9, 2000.

Choudhury, S.B. 1989. "On Udayanchal Movement," in B.C. Bhuyan (ed.), *Political Development of the North-East,* Vol. 1, Delhi: Omsons Publication.

Chowdhury, Mandira Dutta. 2002. "Causes and Remedies of Migration Inside and Into the Barak Valley". Paper presented at the Regional Seminar on "Internally Displaced Persons in Barak Valley" organized by the Department of Political Science, Assam University, on March 27, 2002.

Hussain, Monirul, 2000, "State, Identity Movement and Internal Displacement in the North-East", *Economic and Political Weekly.* Vol. XXXV No. 51: 4519-23.

—. 1994. "The Tribal Question in Assam: A Sociological Appraisal, in Milton S. Sangma (ed.), *Essays on North-East India.* New Delhi: Indus Publishing Company, pp. 278-93.

—. 1989. "Tribal Movement for Autonomous State in Assam", in B.C. Bhuyan (ed.), *Political Development of the North-East,* Vol. 1, Delhi: Omsons Publication.

Imchen, C.L. 1993. "Naga Politics: Regionalism or Non-State Nation?" in B. Pakem (ed.), *Regionalism in India.* New Delhi: Har-Anand Publications, pp. 103-12.

Mazumdar, D.N. 1993. "Ethnicity and Regionalism in North-East India", in B. Pakem (ed.), *Regionalism in India.* New Delhi: Har-Anand Publications, pp. 265-72.

Nag, Sajal. 1990. *Roots of Ethnic Conflict: Nationality Question in North-East India,* New Delhi: Manohar.

—. 2001. "Nationhood and Displacement in Indian Subcontinent", *Economic and Political Weekly.* Vol. XXXVI No. 5c 1: 4753-60.

Nair, Bhaskar. 1989. "Leadership and Role of Political Parties in the North-East", in B.C. Bhuyan (ed.), *Political Development of the North-East,* Vol.1, Delhi: Omsons Publication.

Oommen, T.K. 1993. "Insiders and Outsiders in India: Primordial Collectivities in Nation Building", in Yogesh Atal (ed.), *Understanding Indian Society.* New Delhi: Har-Anand Publications. pp. 454-478.

Pakem, B. 1993. "Nationality Question in the Hill Areas of North-East India", in B. Pakem (ed.), *Regionalism in India.* New Delhi: Har-Anand Publications, pp. 323-33.

Sharma, Manorama. 1990. *Social and Economic Change in Assam: Middle Class Hegemony.* Delhi: Ajanta Publications.

Srikanth, H. 1999. "Communalising Assam: AGP's Loss is BJP's Gain", *Economic and Political Weekly,* December 4, 1999: 3412-14.

Thomas, C.J. 2000. "Resurgence of the Indigenous People in the North-East India: A Case Study of the Youth Movement in the State of Meghalaya". Paper presented at the National Seminar on "Development of STs and SCs in the North-East India in the New Millennium" organized by the Department of Sociology, Assam University, Silchar, December 8-9, 2000.

Thomas, M.M. and Taylor, R.W. 1965. *Tribal Awakening.* Bangalore: Christian Institute for the Study of Religion and Society.

8

Naga Tangle

Is There A Way Out?

KULWINDER KAUR

The Government of India and the NSCN (IM) signed a ceasefire agreement in 1997 to find a solution to the six decade-old Naga problem. Political negotiations have now reached a stage that promises of signing of an accord.[1] These negotiations, not only raise hopes for a lasting solution to the problem, but also many doubts about the outcome of the talks. It is yet to be seen if it leads to a final resolution or pushes Nagaland back into the conflict between the two warring groups. Is the outcome of the negotiations fated as deadlock as has happened with similar negotiations in past? Is complete Naga sovereignty an unrealistic proposition in the present circumstances? Is the right of self-determination an inalienable human right of any nation? There are many more such issues that require attention by all concerned. Perhaps, for the first time in years, a genuine need is felt for a solution. Even the core issue of complete independence is ready to be put on the back burner for lasting peace (Gupta, 2002). The Government of India's recognition of Naga people's uniqueness on July 11, 2002 in a joint communiqué issued from Amsterdam is a departure from its earlier stand.[2] The stage is now set for some hard bargaining. One has to wait and see what kind of peace proposal is finally hammered out (Hussain, 2002).

The main objective of this paper is to examine various issues, which complicate the Naga problem and prepare a balance sheet of factors affecting the ongoing negotiations. These are as under:

1. Emergence of Naga nationality and Indian government's response to it.
2. Are Nagas a group of indigenous people?
3. Is sovereignty an inalienable human right of a collectivity such as Nagas?
4. Is NSCN (IM) the sole and genuine representative of Nagas?
5. Do Manipur, Assam and Arunachal Pradesh have no *locus standi* in the ongoing peace negotiations ?
6. Do past accords and agreements have any significance with regard to the ongoing negotiations?
7. Finally, few facts and conditions having a bearing on the ongoing negotiations have been enlisted.

Before coming to these objectives, it is imperative to locate the Naga people and the land in the broader context of the North-East polity and background.

North-East: A Background

The distinct geomorphology of the North-East has created a condition whereby a social and human geography has evolved over a period of time which is quite distinct from mainland India (Deshpande, 1992: 261-71). Not only is this region surrounded by international borders but also linked to mainland India with only a very narrow strip of land (Ray, 1997: v). In fact, in some respects, the region has been closer to Nepal, Bhutan, Tibet, Myanmar, Bangladesh and other South-East Asian countries than to India. These countries exert sizeable influence on the region (Gopalkrishnan, 1995: xii). Internally, this region is not to be mistaken as uniform, integral, homogeneous or self-conscious. There are circles within circles indicating different levels of mobilization and political consciousness depending upon communality and/or clash of interests at different points of time (Singh, 1987: 1-7). In brief, the region exhibits vertical as well as horizontal divisions. Each as a compartment has its own interactional plane (Gopalkrishnan, 1995: xii).

In the past, people in the North-East lived in different worldviews and there was no consciousness of oneness. Clans used to function as total institutions barring some exchange of items with other tribal groups. It was the interaction of people with the British that sowed the seeds of present-day making of the North-East at the political level. The British interests in the region were: (i) timber, (ii) tea, (iii) oil, (iv) strategic, and (v) Shillong (Deshpande, 1992: 262). Their interaction was skewed with various tribal groups. They adopted the policy of least administration with respect to certain groups of tribals such as Nagas, Abhors, Daflas, Lushai etc. Things such as Inner Line Permit (ILP) of 1873 were devised to isolate the hill tribals from the people of plains/India. The seemingly noble stated object of ILP and other such instruments in reality was exploitative and anti-India in nature (Kumar, 1994: 3; Kumar, 1996: 9-11). Along with the British came the Christian missionaries whose sole objective was to convert the local indigenous population into Christianity.

The post-independence Government of India's response towards the North-East owes a great deal to the developments in the region during the 1940s. There were three main ideas at that time regarding the future of the North-East region in free India. The first view was to retain this as a 'Hill Colony' under the British Empire. The logic behind this was to safeguard the rights of indigenous people of this region against the assimilative tendency of mainstream Indian population. The another idea was propagated by some political leaders of the North-East with the British support who wanted independence of their respective regions from Indian government. The third view was that of the Indian political leadership who viewed itself as the natural inheritor of British legacy in Indian subcontinent. The Indian political leadership was quite assertive and they did not allow the British to succeed in their designs of creating a 'Crown Colony'. The Constituent Assembly Sub-Committee (Bordoloi Committee), while recommending the safeguards for tribal and indigenous people to be included in the Constitution of India, in effect, desired to have them integrated ultimately with the mainland people through the democratic processes. However, the assumption underlying the intended integration of various communities in the North-East with Assam and subsequently with mainstream India was also not free from weaknesses. In fact, the post-independence period has much to say on this count.

After independence, introduction of panchayati raj institutions, autonomous district councils, autonomous councils with more than one districts, state within the state (e.g., Meghalaya in Assam in 1970) etc. though made the North-East a veritable laboratory of experiments, yet most of the tribal people were not satisfied with their political status. The question of Assamese as an official language created a feeling of mutual mistrust among various tribal/ethnic groups in the region and alienated the people not only from Assamese society but also from the Central Government (Trivedi, 1995:xv; Choudhury, 1989: 103-26). The result was the reorganization of the North-East in 1972. Even the process of fragmentation of the North-East failed to satisfy the aspirations of various ethnic groups such as Bodos and other plain tribal groups as is evident in post-1972 North-East (Bhuyan, 1989: vii). Gopalkrishnan points out that ethnicity, language and religion have in recent years become extremely strong forces playing consequential role in the stability and integration of the region (1995: 176).

In post-1947 era, North-East part of India is perhaps a region which has undergone maximum metamorphosis in this part of the world (Singh, 1987: 1-7). The Centre had to face maximum numbers of ethnic movements, revolts, militancy, and insurgencies. Many overground and underground organizations cropped up in this region. The question of Naga insurgency remained quite disturbing throughout the second half of this century. The region earned a bad image of being a 'nest of insurgents' (Trivedi, 1995:xv; Choudhury, 1989: 103-26). In this background, we shall now examine the Naga people and their problems in greater detail.

Naga Ethnicity: Tribe to Nation

Anthropologically, Naga is an umbrella nomenclature given to a particular conglomeration of segmented tribal groups located on the north-eastern frontier of India. In the nineteenth century, these tribal groups were not aware of each other and their worldview was limited to their village and nearby *jhum* cultivation areas. Headhunting, animism and inter-tribal conflicts were quite prevalent in this part of the frontier. There was no concept of Naga or Nagaland among these inhabitants as development was yet to begin. Politically, neither the Nagas nor this part of territory was under the control of any power till 1880. Before this, till 1832, the Ahoms had relations with Nagas but they never had any effective control over the Naga territory. The British too did not gain any effective control till 1880. This feeling of separateness from the rest of the India is so widely shared by the Nagas that it may be considered as one of the prime forces in their long struggle against a powerful adversary (Mishra, 1988: 2; Gopalkrishnan, 1995: 30-51).

Though, politically, the Naga area was gradually brought under the control of the British, they left it to the inhabitants as far as management of their internal affairs and local democracy was concerned (Mishra, 1988: 2). The ILP under the 1873 regulation came into operation and no Indian from the plain areas could enter into the territory for any purpose whatsoever without a permit from a competent authority. In this way, the

British succeeded in keeping the Nagas cut off from the rest of the subcontinent and they remained practically untouched by the forces of Indian nationalism.

The British advancement in the region brought with it missionaries to work in the Naga territory. American Baptist missionaries arrived in this part of India in early nineteenth century and began working in the area of education and health and through that they changed the inhabitants' worldview (Sinha, 1994: 69-90). By the end of the nineteenth century, majority of the inhabitants started practising Christianity. This process continued during the twentieth century as well. Headhunting was gradually stopped in the area under the influence of Christianity. The number of inter-village and inter-tribal feuds also fell down. Church and missionary schools became a melting pot for Naga culture. A nascent pan-Naga feeling started emerging among the educated, middle class Naga Christian youth (Mishra, 1988: 21-30; Gopalkrishnan, 1995: 30-51).

Naga Nation and the Demand for Naga Sovereignty (1919 to 1947)

In the twentieth century, the educated Naga youths were recruited in the British Army and a contingent of 5,000 Naga youths went as far as France as a part of British Army in the World War I. They were greatly influenced by the spirit of the rise of the nationalism in many countries of the world that they witnessed during the war (Ao, 2002: 40-45). Back home, they felt the need for unification of Naga inhabitants and started thinking about the future course for Nagas as it was clear by that time that the British were going to leave India one day. The same batch of Nagas founded the Naga Club in 1918 and paved the way for Naga nationalism and patriotism. It was the beginning of unification of Naga tribes and subsequently emerged as a struggle for Naga nationality. The Naga Club leadership believed in the uniqueness of Naga history and culture.

They got an opportunity to press their demands through Simon Commission in 1929 when it visited Kohima in Nagaland. In its memorandum, submitted to the Simon Commission, the Naga Club demanded that Naga people be left to themselves as and when the British eventually left this country. More than 20 representatives from different tribes signed this document. In spite of the fact that this move by the Naga Club yielded no results, it must be noted that this was the first ever collective move on the part of leading individuals from different tribes to spell out their view on the future of Naga people (Mishra, 1988: 6).

During the 1930s, the emergence of Naga nationalism became quite strong as was evident from Zeliang Movement and it got further impetus during the World War II when Naga people again gave support to the British Army against its enemies. The World War II brought Nagaland to the centre stage of the world and quite aware of this the Naga elites expected the British to give them independence in return of their support and help. The decade of 1940s was momentous in the history of the British, the Indians as well as the Nagas. The Naga people were quite excited by the expected changes in the subcontinent. C.R. Pawsey, the then Deputy Commissioner of the Naga district of Assam, invited Nagas to discuss the future issues at Kohima and paved the way for the formation of the Naga Hills District Tribal Council in 1945. Various rounds of discussions regarding the future of Naga people held, which led to the creation of Naga National Council (NNC) in 1946. The NNC had 29 members representing various tribes on the principle of proportional representation and for the first time in history the Naga people were coming under a single political organization (Mishra, 1988: 7).

It was the NNC which has been spearheading the demand of Naga sovereignty since 1946 onwards. The leadership of

NNC submitted a number of petitions, prayers and memorandums to various authorities for complete Naga sovereignty. This demand did not find any support from either the British or the Indian leadership. Jawaharlal Nehru absolutely ruled out any such eventuality in a letter written to NNC leader, T. Sakhrie and subsequently in 1946 when Naga leadership met him in Delhi. Mahatma Gandhi and C. Rajagopalachari, however, were not in favour of forceful integration of Naga territory into India. Nehru, nevertheless, remained opposed to any such move on the part of Naga leadership and also warned them in no uncertain terms on this issue. He, however, promised to provide sufficient autonomy to Nagas within the framework of Indian Constitution.

Another significant development took place in 1946 when an agreement was signed between Shri Hyadri, the then Governor of Assam as the British representative and the NNC leadership. This nine-point agreement provided for 10 years' guardianship of Indian government over Naga people on whose expiry, the Naga people were free to remain under the Indian guardianship or to gain sovereignty. However, such an agreement was unacceptable to Nehru and therefore could not be implemented. On August 14, 1947, one day before the country became independent, the Naga leadership unilaterally declared Naga independence day. This was viewed as an act of Naga effrontery by Indian leadership (Tarapot, 1994: 102-26).

The movement led by the NNC, which was aimed at achieving the solidarity of the Naga tribes, contributed immensely towards the lessening of inter-tribal rivalry and the emergence of an all-Naga consciousness, which is today loosely defined as "the Naga way of life". The NNC, through its social and political elements and methods of organization, paved the way for the emergence of the modern Naga nation. Prior to this, most of the tribes lived in isolation and the role of the tribal council was limited to the 'village republics' (Mishra, 1988: 30). He further points out that the Naga loyalty to his tribe or clan was gradually replaced by his loyalty to the concept of United Nagaland or Greater Nagaland. And, the demand for Greater Nagaland was clearly linked with the growing tide of Naga nationalism, which had succeeded in greatly reducing, if not altogether doing away with, inter-tribe and inter-clan rivalry.

Indian Government Response

Under Phizo's leadership, the NNC was transformed into a militant political organization wedded to the idea of a sovereign Nagaland. The NNC rejected the Sixth Schedule of the Indian Constitution. It was assumed by Indian political leadership that democratic processes such as universal adult franchise, regular general elections for parliament and assembly, planned development through five-year plans and community development, guarantee of autonomy to backward tribal communities through the District Autonomous Council (DAC) within the Sixth Schedule of Constitution of India, and protection of human rights through constitutional guarantees, will remove the misgivings of all the ethnicities of the North-East and other parts of India. It was also assumed that Naga people's socio-economic and political aspirations would be fulfilled through the above mentioned processes and that they would be integrated with the Indian mainstream in general and the North-East culture in particular. But, Naga people continued on a collision path. They declared their independence in 1947 on 14th August, adopted a national anthem and separate constitution, formed their own government and intimated the outside world about it. They refused to accept the sovereignty of India over Nagaland. In the year 1950, Phizo, the unrivalled theoretician of sovereign Nagaland, was unanimously elected President of the Naga National Council. Thereafter, NNC boycotted the elections to the Naga District Autonomous Council held for the first time in independent India. They also boycotted the general elections held on January 25, 1951 despite persuasion by the central and Assam governments. In 1951, fuelled by a successful Civil Disobedience Movement, all the Nagas under the leadership of Phizo held a plebiscite for Naga sovereignty.

The Indian government refused to take the plebiscite seriously as it was estimated to be conducted under duress. Another incident took place on March 30, 1953 when both Nehru and Myanmar Premier, Thakin Nu (Unu) visited Kohima to understand the Naga issue. The Nagas that pushed both the parties to the battleground boycotted their public meeting. Thousands of young Nagas joined the Naga Home Guard and almost the entire NNC set-up went underground (Mishra 1988: 9). By now, the Government of India had begun to view Naga problem as a law and order issue and hence chances of negotiated settlement became bleak (Ao, 2002: 5). The Indian Army started conducting operations to counter insurgency. On March 22, 1956, the NNC declared its complete independence and formed Government of Federal Nagaland as per Hyadri Agreement of 1946, which was not honoured by the Indian government. Counter-insurgency operations were intensified and allegations of violations of human rights started cropping up from both the sides. Once again, the Naga people boycotted the general elections in 1957. In brief, neither democratic processes nor planned development took off in Nagaland. The consequence was the suffering of common masses. The human rights were relegated to the background.

Similar to every other resistance movement, the Naga movement too has various shades of ideologies and methods of agitation. It is divided into two groups—the moderates and the extremists. Of these, the moderate group wanted resolution through peaceful means within the framework of Indian Constitution. Long-drawn negotiations between moderates led by Naga Peoples Convention (NPC) and the Indian government led to signing of a sixteen-point agreement in 1960 under which a new state of Nagaland was created in 1963. It was for the first time that linguistic principle was ignored for territorial reorganization of Indian states. The newly formed state was to fulfil the aspirations of Naga people for autonomy and freedom. The move of Indian government did succeed in mitigating the demands of sovereignty to some extent. However, the Naga insurgents read it as a trap laid down by Indian government with the aid of Naga traitors to confuse the Naga people and intensified their activities (Mishra, 1988: 10). Meanwhile, in 1960, Phizo reached London to internationalize the issue.

It was for the first time in 1964 that the Indian government realized the futility of treating the Naga problem as a law and order problem and instead felt the need to address it at political level. This realization led to signing of a ceasefire agreement on September 4, 1964 with provisions for periodic extensions. Talks at the highest level continued till six rounds of negotiations. The Naga leadership was offered complete autonomy except the defence, external affairs, communications and currency by the then Indian Prime Minister, Indira Gandhi. But, it refused the offer and stuck to its demand for complete sovereignty. Hence, the talks reached a deadlock.

In 1975, an agreement was signed in Shillong between the representatives of underground organizations, authorized by Naga National Council, and the Indian government to reach a final solution to the problem within the framework of Indian Constitution. This time the NNC and its leader Phizo did not criticize it. But it was not acceptable to many Naga people since it tacitly accepted Indian sovereignty and led to surrender of arms and ammunition. The Naga leadership alleged that the Naga signatories to it were, in reality, Naga traitors. The reaction was vehement and it led the leadership to revolt against Phizo and formation of a separate organization under the name of National Socialist Council of Nagaland (NSCN) on January

31, 1980. Since its inception, this organization has been leading a virtual war against Indian Army. The latter had to operate extensively to counter its activities. The NSCN, in fact, has developed into and turned out be the most powerful underground organization operating in North-East India (Tarapot, 1994: 111). The masses, all this while, had been sandwiched between the two warring groups. For almost five decades now, the people of Nagaland have not breathed in peace, let alone, realized their human rights. The Naga insurgents themselves are not a united group and factional killings are going on for last five decades. It is believed that in 1988, Isac and Muivah, the two top leaders of NSCN, wanted to solve Naga problem by accepting an autonomous state within Indian Union. But nothing less than sovereignty was acceptable to Khaplang. As a result, NSCN saw a vertical split leading to formation of two factions—NSCN (IM) and NSCN (K)—in 1988 and these two factions are active in Manipur and Myanmar area respectively. However, amongst the two, the NSCN (IM) is more organized.

Ongoing Negotiations: Issues and Possibilities

Various rounds of talks between the Government of India and the NSCN (IM) leadership have been conducted at Amsterdam, Bangkok, and Osaka. It is claimed by NSCN Chairman Isaac Swu that the "Government of India recognises the unique history and situation of the Nagas". This declaration is a part of a joint communique issued on July 11, 2002 (*Assam Tribune*, August 18, 2002:7). The Central Government is also contemplating to lift the ban imposed on NSCN (IM) to facilitate the talks. There is excitement and hope for a final solution so that peace can return to the Nagas.

At this point, it is pertinent to briefly state about the conflict between India and Nagaland. Ao (2002) has very succinctly summarized it. The underlying philosophy of the conflict, as given by Ao, firstly, takes Nagas to be a group of indigenous people who have been artificially divided by drawing arbitrary lines by imperialist forces against their wishes. Secondly, it believes sovereignty to be their inalienable human right. These assumptions of Naga people complicate the problem and make it difficult to find out a solution acceptable to all the stakeholders in the issue. Sovereignty issue may lead to deadlock as it happened in 1967 when Naga were offered a sort of complete autonomy except defence, external affairs, communications and currency with India. To put the issues in a proper perspective, we would examine the following points in the given order:

1. Nagas' claim as an indigenous nation
2. Naga sovereignty as a human rights issue
3. The divided Naga house
4. Greater Nagaland and apprehensions of Assam, Manipur and Arunachal Pradesh
5. Past accords, agreements and peace proposals

Are Nagas an Indigenous People?

The National Socialist Council of Nagaland (NSCN) and other Naga organizations have been claiming that the Nagas are a group of indigenous people who are sandwiched between China, Myanmar and India. The geographical spread as per their claim lies in between the latitudes 23° 5' and 28° 3' North and longitudes 93° and 97° East (Ao, 2002: 248). Nagas belong to Mongoloid race and have a distinct history, culture and polity. They are neither Indian nor Chinese. They do not feel anything common with Indians and refuse to be clubbed with rest of the tribal Indians and for that matter with others in the world. They are an independent and proud nation since time immemorial and have never been conquered by any one. They have been arbitrarily divided in states within India and

Myanmar. Like any other nation, they admit to internal heterogeneity, being comprised of forty different tribes with distinct cultural identities. However, all these different tribes shared a distinct history and have sense of belongingness to a pan-Naga identity. In brief, the Nagas are a separate nation of indigenous people, who have been forcefully subjugated by Indian Army.

At the international level, the Naga protagonists have been clamouring for their recognition as indigenous/autochthonous people. Due to their sustained efforts, the Nagas under the leadership of Isaac Chisi Swu and T. Muivah acquired membership of Unrepresented Nations and Peoples Organizations (UNPO) in 1993 (Ao, 2002: 67). Some other international agencies are also supporting the claim and cause of Naga people for quite some time. Recognition of Naga people as a nation as well as an indigenous people has certain political ramifications. Indigenous nations have a right of self-determination which is the ultimate right of any indigenous group. The Naga peoples, too, claim that self-determination is their inalienable group human right and they are leading the resistance movement against the forceful occupation of their territory by India and Myanmar.

The Government of India, on the other hand, denies the existence of any indigenous population in India. It also concedes that due to geographical and social isolation over a period of time, certain groups of people have lagged behind in development. In order to bring such groups at par, the government has initiated certain affirmative measures. The Nagas are also a group of numerous tribals situated in North-East India and they are distinct in culture yet an integral part of Indian society and polity. They have been given sufficient autonomy, as per Indian Constitution, to enjoy all cultural and other rights and also to preserve their distinct identity. In brief, the Indian government dismisses the claim of Nagas as being indigenous population.

Is Naga Sovereignty a Human Rights Issue?

The most vital point of conflict is Naga sovereignty vs. Indian Constitution. As stated above, Nagas have been claiming that sovereignty is their inalienable collective human right. The Indian government treats Naga territory and Naga people as an integral part of India. Any movement that challenges the sovereignty of Indian Constitution is treated as separatist or secessionist. In the past, numerous ethnic movements have emerged but found solution to their problems within the framework of the Constitution of India. Therefore, any ethnic movement that has any perceived or imagined or real grievances have to be redressed within the framework of Indian Constitution. In brief, whosoever claims that Naga people are not a part of Indian State, is treated as secessionist. This issue needs re-examination in the light of theory of human rights.

Human rights are a set of inalienable socio-economic, political and other rights of any human being admissible to him/her by virtue of being a member of mankind. Are these rights absolute in nature and to be provided at any cost to collectivity? Do these sets of rights include right of self-determination as the ultimate political right of any nationality? Let us assume that self-determination is an inalienable human right of any nationality. It, then, has implications for world political map leading to the fragmentation of existing political units. As a consequence, the whole world would be divided into thousands of political units. Presently, the world is full of multi-nation-states since there are hardly any nation-states left in the classical sense of the term. The multi-nation-state is, in fact, universal and is supported by Phadnis (1989), Oommen (1997), Karna (1999) and Segal (2002). Every state includes many nations and each nation is having multiple sub-nationalities within it. If we keep applying the logic of self-determination as an unalienable human right of a nationality, it would lead to endless cycles of segmentation and, hence, anarchy. The state, therefore, has been devised by humanity to manage the affairs of a sizeable amount of population in a given territorial jurisdiction. Conversely, the state has to address itself to the grievances, complaints and human rights of all the constituent nationalities, classes etc. to acquire legitimacy. Any demand for separation or secession, therefore, has to be evaluated in this background.

The world needs a minimum of *homeostatic* for its existence and any politico-administrative reorganization should contribute towards this balance rather than leading to further disintegration, instability or anomie. Therefore, right to self-determination cannot be said to be absolute; it cannot be granted at the cost of territorial integration, political stability and state sovereignty. It has to be examined in a specific context. However, it goes without saying that human rights must be guaranteed to all individuals and nationalities residing within a state. Equality, equity and justice must be practised in dealing with all the constituent units. The constitution of a state should be flexible enough to accommodate the genuine demands and aspirations of any particular nationality. An empirical enquiry into today's world political map would validate the proposition that the contemporary states are multiple nation-states and every nationality is further made up of sub-nationalities. The opinion in the theory as well as practice of polity in the world is not in favour of considering right to self-determination as absolute right of any nationality. It is also true that nationalities, ethnicities, nation-states or state-nations are not fixed categories and are always in the process of making. It would be more appropriate to call them as processes rather than structures. The Nagas of today are not the same as they were hundred years ago. They have changed and done so irreversibly. Likewise, their demand of sovereignty may, under a given set of circumstances, seem undesirable.

This leads to the other point of view which states that only in case a particular nationality is discriminated against, or exploited, or forcefully assimilated/annihilated, or genocide is attempted, or human rights of individuals are violated, either by some dominant nationality or by some vested interests or some particular government for a sufficiently long time, can the right of 'self-determination' be invoked by that nationality for its survival. In such a case, world opinion definitely favours such demand. Have Naga people been treated in this manner in India is a question, which can be empirically and historically examined. Have there been any serious attempts by the Naga leaders to address such issues of assimilation, cultural invasion, or economic exploitation through peaceful or democratic means to the concerned competent authorities? Have all the moves of reconciliation for remaining within Indian State been exhausted? If yes, they have a right to demand cession. If not, it can best be considered either a demand by vested interests or attempt by foreign powers to destabilize India. Are Naga people unanimous in their resolution and technique. If not, it cannot be said to be a popular demand and at best be described as politically motivated.

It is very essential to examine whether the sovereignty is a prior condition for existence or people have other fundamental issues of existence to address such as socio-economic backwardness, poverty, unemployment, ethnic identity and so on. If there were such issues to address, what has been the response of Central Government to them? Has Central Government been discriminatory and exploitative or has it taken keen interest to remove these problems? It also needs to be examined as to what has been done by the government to ensure cultural distinctiveness, ethnic identity, self-respect, autonomy of management of social affairs of that community, and devolution of decision-making and political power to the grassroots level. All these questions need to be examined before accepting or rejecting any demand for self-determination by any nationality. Indian government claims to have tried its utmost to address the genuine grievances of all ethnicities including the Nagas. In conclusion, unlike self-determination, sovereignty is not an absolute and inalienable human right of any nationality.

Are Nagas Unanimous in their Resolve?

The Nagas are divided among themselves in their resolve about a final solution to the problem. There are numerous groups and we see no consensus among them. In the past, the Naga National Council (NNC) started struggle for sovereignty but Naga Peoples Convention (NPC) accepted Indian sovereignty and state of Nagaland was created in 1963 to fulfil the genuine aspirations of the people. The creation of Nagaland was considered as political trap by the Naga rebels and the fight continued. The Shillong Accord of 1975 was signed by a delegation of representatives of Naga underground organizations and Indian government. It was considered a betrayal of Naga interests and led to formation of National Socialish Council of Nagaland (NSCN) in 1980. Subsequently, in 1988, NSCN was further divided into Isaac-Muivah (IM) and Khaplang (K) factions over the issue of settlement with Indian government. This made them kill each other's cadre and this fratricidal killing is going on as yet. In spite of reconciliation move by Naga Hoho, Naga Church and Naga Mothers Association, the fight is on in various areas between the cadres of two factions. The recent killing of NSCN (K) cadre by NSCN (IM) cadre is a living testimony of it. The NNC, too, has two factions and there are no chances of reconciliation between the two.

The Nagaland government is also an important player and the Congress government led by S.C. Jamir demanded a solution based on the sixteen-point agreement of 1960 which, according to it, is the 'Bedrock of Naga People Movement'. S.C. Jamir the then Chief Minister categorically ruled out the need for sovereignty since autonomy within Indian Constitution was sufficient to meet the aspirations of people provided the NSCN stopped extortion, coercion and false propaganda. His government was toying with the idea of Greater Nagaland by acquiring some areas from Manipur, Assam and Arunachal Pradesh. Incidently, Jamir was a signatory to the sixteen-point agreement of 1960. The NSCN (IM) considered him the biggest hurdle in the peace process and vehemently condemned his recently published controversial booklet 'Bedrock of Naga People Movement' in which he had justified the 1960 agreement. The Naga people are living in a state of confusion. In addition to this, inter-tribal differences and clashes are not uncommon either. In brief, the differences among two factions of NSCN are quite significant and no single group can claim to be the sole representative of the Naga people. The Naga villages have become the breeding centres of infighting amongst themselves, siding different overground and underground governments. The Nagas on their part are confused and fed up with these para-governments (Ao, 2002: 91). In reality, the Nagas are fighting amongst themselves in the name of 'Nagaland for Christ'.

The ongoing talks are suffering from this limitation as neither the NNC nor NSCN(K) is a party to it. The third Naga Consultation Meet held at Bangkok in May 2002 to thrash out ways to strengthen the peace strategy called upon all Nagas to unite and participate in the ongoing peace negotiations. Attended by as many as 73 Naga groups, apart from representatives from Manipur, Assam and Arunachal Pradesh, it concluded with a four-point formal declaration: (i) to fully support the political negotiations between NSCN (IM) and Indian government, (ii) Naga Hoho, churches and NGOs ought to bring about Naga unity, (iii) all Nagas should participate in the peace process, and (iv) Naga churches should hold a

National Prayer Day for attaining the above objectives (Dewan, 2002). It further emphasized on reconciliation between various Naga groups on the principle of forgive and forget.

Greater Nagaland and Apprehensions of Assam, Manipur and Arunachal

The politico-administrative developments since the British advent of this part of India, and more particularly after independence, have transformed the region substantially. It has brought about certain changes which are irreversible and their ignorance may lead to incalculable damage to peace and stability of the whole region. The area being called Greater Nagaland or Nagalim falls in addition to Nagaland in Manipur, Assam and Arunachal Pradesh. This is being resented by these states. Neighbouring states of Manipur, Assam and Arunachal Pradesh are not being made a party to the peace talks, hence, they have reasons for keeping apprehensions about the outcome of talks. The people of these states desire peace in the region but not at the cost of their own peace and territory. They have a grudge against the Central Government for keeping them in the dark about the details of the negotiations. It may not be realistic to form Greater Nagaland or Nagalim in the present scenario as it has a potential to disintegrate the whole of North-East India. No state is willing to give any territory to the Nagas for what they call 'Naga expansionism' or 'Naga invasion'.

Manipur is most assertive over this issue. The incidents of June 2001 after the extension of ceasefire between the NSCN (IM) and Union Government on 14 June 2001 'without territorial limitation' are yet fresh in the memory of the people. The Manipur Legislative Assembly, has on six occasions passed unanimous resolutions against territorial disintegration of

Manipur. In its last resolution of June 14, 2002 it had urged the Union Government to amend Article 3 of Indian Constitution to provide for territorial sanctity of Manipur. Similarly, respective governments and people of Assam and Arunachal Pradesh have also made it clear that any move towards reorganization in favour of Nagaland would not be tolerated.

In August 2002, the State Assembly of Arunachal Pradesh, too, had passed a unanimous resolution by calling the Centre for amending the Article 3 of Indian Constitution for ensuring territorial integrity of Arunachal Pradesh. The resolution made it quite clear that Arunachal Pradesh is not a party to the Centre and NSCN (IM) peace negotiations and it should not be dragged into the same. The government and people of Arunachal are highly critical of NSCN (IM)'s claims that some tribal groups in their state are Nagas. Arunachal considers such claims as outrageous. Besides, there are already enough disputes among north-eastern states on the issues of boundary, some of them are even pending in the Supreme Court. In brief, the issue of Greater Nagaland is a very sensitive one and is probably the biggest hurdle in the peace process.

Past Accords, Agreements and Peace Proposals

History reveals that each agreement signed so far turned out to be a political mockery creating confusion, division and destruction of Naga society (Ao, 2002: 89). Since independence in 1947, various efforts have been made by both parties to settle the issue but all in vain. The most important agreements signed between the two parties are the Hyadri agreement of 1946, sixteen-point agreement of 1960 and the Shillong accord of 1975. The Hyadri agreement provided for ten years' guardianship of India over Naga area and after the expiry of which the Naga people were free to either extend that guardianship or declare their independence. The agreement was signed between the then Governor of Assam and the NNC leadership. Nehru rejected it outrightly which became a cause of a lot of resentment among the Nagas. The NNC, out of pique, declared independence on August 14, 1947.

The second agreement was signed between the Naga People Convention (NPC) and the Centre in 1960 and it led to the formation of a separate state of Nagaland in 1963. It is popularly known as sixteen-point agreement and the creation of Nagaland was just a part of it. Incidentally, the then Chief Minister, S.C. Jamir was one of the signatories to it. This agreement was not acceptable to the NNC and other Naga leaders as they felt that the NPC has compromised the Naga interests and sovereignty by signing this accord. It was also alleged that the NPC was a body without any Naga mandate mainly comprising *Dubhasiyas* and government servants who were keen to please the Centre and thus fell a pray to Indian designs. For Naga rebels Nagaland state was a trap created by the Indian government to confuse the Naga people and the world.

The most controversial of all agreements was signed in 1975 between representatives of NNC and the Centre at Shillong. As per this agreement, the Nagas accepted the Indian sovereignty unconditionally and surrendered some arms. This again was not acceptable to many Nagas but significantly no criticism of the agreement came from Phizo. The other leaders, namely, Isaac, Muivah and Khaplang waited, in vain, for Phizo to respond. Phizo's silence impelled the second rung leadership of Nagas to organize themselves against the Shillong accord under the banner of National Socialist Council of Nagalim (NSCN) in 1980.

Over the last six decades various proposals have been put forward from different quarters to solve the Naga problem. Most of them projected either Naga rebels or of Indian government's viewpoint. Only a few have been made out of a genuine concern to solve the Naga tangle after giving due consideration to the concerns of both the parties. Ao (2002) has described various proposals in detail, of which three merit mention here. These are: Indira Gandhi's proposal (1967), Uncle Suiza's proposal of 1967 and 1971 and Longkumar's proposal.

In 1967, the then Foreign Minister, Dinesh Singh, on behalf of Indira Gandhi, offered complete autonomy to Nagas except for the departments of defence, foreign affairs, communications and currency. It was a very serious proposal but Nagas could not understand its import at that time. Uncle Suiza also proposed that there could be a common link between India and Nagas on certain subjects like defence, foreign affairs, communications and so on under the guardianship of India. He further elaborated his proposal and pointed out that India and Nagaland can have separate constitutions as well as political entities maintaining separate nations under a common union. Similarly, Longkumar, in his famous write up 'The Naga Question', opined that the integration of Naga inhabited areas with autonomy and home rule by NNC within the Indian Union could be a middle ground to solve the Indo-Naga problem. By 'home rule' he meant control over all the departments except defence, foreign, and communications while residual powers rest with Nagaland. He wanted a federal relationship of American type with double citizenship, constitution, judiciary and administrative system etc. with greater devolution of powers. None of the three proposals, unfortunately, could be examined seriously by both the parties.

Is There a Way Out?

Notwithstanding the ongoing talks between the Indian government and NSCN (IM) leadership the problem of Naga people's demand for a separate Naga country remains as daunting as it was 58 years ago on the eve of Indian independence. During this period, India has witnessed various other ethnic movements as well, with different levels of mobilization, spread and intensity. Unlike the Naga problem, in majority of the cases, a national policy of liberal, just and flexible constitution, universal adult suffrage, economic development, politico-administrative reorganization and devolution of political powers to people through grassroots democratic institutions was able to resolve these conflicts based on ethnicity. The Constitution of India provided desirable safeguards to religious and linguistic minorities as well as socio-geographically isolated population in the country. Be it the problem of Tamil or Punjabi ethnicity, the Telengana, Mizo, Assamese or Bodo demands, all have been tackled within the framework of Indian Constitution.

A cursory survey of various ethnic resistance movements, which emerged in post-independence India, lends credence to the theory that ethnicity is an ongoing process in a multi-racial, multi-cultural, multi-linguistic and multi-religious society like India (Phadnis, 1989). North-East India has witnessed the maximum number of secessionist movements with a growth of over one hundred underground militant organizations questioning the Indian sovereignty. Some of these movements were dealt as a law and order problem, while others were tackled through political negotiations and yet others through a combination of the two. It is correct to state that the issue of Nagaland had been a *Gordian knot* (emphasis mine) right from the beginning of Indian independence (ibid: 91). Before any accord is signed as an outcome of the ongoing negotiations, it would be worthwhile to keep the following few facts and conditions in mind:

1. All the concerned parties must agree to the point that it is essentially a political problem and there cannot be any military solution to it. Military actions by both the parties in the past have led to unnecessary killings, maiming and torturing of thousands of innocent people.
2. All the concerned parties must realize that colonial occupation of Indian territory had set in certain changes in all the aspects of socio-economic, administrative and economic reality of India which are irreversible. Making of

present-day India, and especially North-East, is to be understood in totality and not in a segmented way. Indian strategic concerns cannot be ignored. Similarly, human rights of any nationality, too, must be respected.

3. Any settlement between the Centre and the Nagas must involve all the underground organizations. It must be broad-based and debated among the Nagas or else it may turn out to be another dead document of history.
4. The people of Manipur, Assam and Arunachal Pradesh must be taken into confidence and made a party to negotiations if any territorial reorganization is involved in the settlement. If wishes of people of these states are ignored, the whole peace process will be jeopardized.
5. Genuine demand of Nagas for a Greater Nagaland is to be examined honestly by the Centre. Manipur, Assam and Arunachal Pradesh should also examine this with an open mind. The principle of give and take can be applied in this regard and slight adjustments in the larger interest must be made to overcome the tangle.
6. Greater autonomy to Nagaland must be given to fulfil the 'national' aspirations of Nagas. The American or Canadian type of federation with double citizenship could be explored by making some extraordinary constitutional provisions.
7. The Nagas, too, ought to approach the problem with an open mind and any insistence on sovereignty will again lead to deadlock and bloodshed. The draft proposals must be discussed in the entire country and Naga organizations must play an active role and allout efforts must be made for Naga reconciliation and unification.
8. For the first time, the two parties are talking to each other without any pre-conditions. It is a welcome departure from the earlier times. It all shows that both the parties have started appreciating each other's viewpoint.

9. The Centre's acceptance of uniqueness of Naga history and identity is a definite pointer that both the parties are adopting an open mind towards the issue.

The ongoing negotiations provide an opportunity to approach this issue with an open mind by all concerned parties. Not only lessons must be learnt from the history but the changed circumstances must also be appreciated. Any insistence on unrealistic conditions would only pave the way for the deadlock and subsequent suffering to the Naga people.

Notes

1. "The Naga leaders' decision to hold talks in India is a sure sign of progress", said N. Krome, the Secretary of the Naga Peoples' Movement for Human Rights. He further said, "May be the two sides are beginning to trust each other. Hence, such a flexible approach" (Hussain, 2002). The President of Naga Mothers Association opined that our need for peace is more important than our desire for independence and sovereignty (Gupta, 2002).
2. The Government of India is actively contemplating to lift the ban imposed on NSCN(IM) for creating a congenial atmosphere for next round of negotiations likely to be held in India.

References

Ao, A.L. 2002. *From Phizo to Muivah: The Naga National Question*. New Delhi: Mittal Publications.

Bhuyan, A.C. 1989. "The Ahom-Naga Relations (1228 to 1838 AD)" in B.C. Bhuyan (ed.), *Political Development of the North-East.* New Delhi: Omsons Publications.

—. (ed.) 1989. *Political Development of the North-East*. New Delhi: Omsons Publications.

Choudhury, S.B. 1989. "On Udayachal Movement" in B.C. Bhuyan (ed.), *Political Development of the North-East*. New Delhi: Omsons Publications.

Chaube, S.K. 1985. *Electoral Politics in North East India*. Madras: University Press.

Datta, P.S. (ed.) 1993. *Autonomy Movements in Assam (Documents)*. New Delhi: Omsons Publications

—. (ed.) 1995. *North-East and the Indian State: Paradoxes of a Periphery*. New Delhi: Vikas.

Deshpande, C.D. 1992. *India: A Regional Interpretation*. New Delhi: ICSSR.

Dewan, D. 2002. "Bangkok Consultation Meet: Renewed Mandate", *North-East Sun*, Vol. 7, No. 21.

Dutta, P.S. 1996. *Electoral Politics in North-East India*. New Delhi: Omsons.

Elwin, Verrier. 1969. *The Nagas in the 19th Century (Anthology)*. Bombay: Oxford University Press.

Gopalkrishnan, R. 1995. *Insurgency North-Eastern Region of India*. New Delhi: Vikas Publishing House Pvt. Ltd.

Gupta, Sujay. 2002. "Talks and Theatric as Jamir's Magic Fails", *Times of India*. Kolkata, 26 August.

—. 2002. "Hues of Naga Unity Rainbow", *Times of India*. Kolkata, 20 August.

Hussain, Seema. 2002. "Farewell to Arms", *The Week*, Vol 20, No.34.

Karna, M.N. 1999. "Language, Region and National Identity", *Sociological Bulletin*, Vol. 48 (1, 2): 75-96.

Kumar, B.B. 1994. *Trends of British Annexation of North-East India*. New Delhi: Omsons.

—. 1996. *Reorganization of North-East India (Facts and Documents)*. New Delhi: Omsons Publications.

Mishra, Udayon. 1988. *North-East India: Quest for Identity*. New Delhi: Omsons Publications.

Morantz, Toby. 1997. "Individual Rights versus Collective Rights: The Debate on the Aboriginal People of Canada", *Sociological Bulletin, Vol. 46(2).*

Oommen, T.K. 1997. *Citizenship, Nationality, and Ethnicity: Reconciling Competing Identities*. Cambridge: Polity Press.

Pakem, B. (ed.) 1997. *Insurgency in North-East India*. New Delhi: Omsons.

—. 1999. *Coalition Politics in North-East India*. New Delhi: Regency Publication.

Phadnis, U. 1989. *Ethnicity and Nation-building in South Asia*. New Delhi: Sage Publications.

Rao, V.V. 1989. "Inter-State Relations: Boundary Dispute in North-East India" in B.C. Bhuyan (ed.), *Political Development of the North-East*. New Delhi: Omsons.

Rao, V.V. and N. Hazarika. 1983. *A Century of Government and Politics in North-East India* (1874-1980), Vol. 1, New Delhi: S. Chand.

Ray, B.D. 1997. "Foreword" in B. Pakem (ed.), *Insurgency in North-East India*. New Delhi: Omsons.

Segal, E.E. 2002. "Intersections Among Tribalism, Ethnicity and Gender in the light of African Data", *Sociological Bulletin*, Vol. 49(1): 1-7.

Singh, B.P. 1987. *The Problem of Change: A Study of North-East India*. New Delhi: Oxford University Press.

Sinha, A.C. 1994. *North-Eastern Frontier of India*. New Delhi: Indus Publishing Company.

Tarapot, P.B. 1994. *Insurgency Movement in North-Eastern India*. New Delhi: Vikas.

Trivedi, U.R. (ed.) 1995. *Documents on Assam*. New Delhi: Omsons Publications.

9

Will to Hate

Gujarat and the Violence of Identity

ANJAN GHOSH

Posing the Problematic

In Ahmedabad, "for the first time, small boys and girls are asking their fathers and uncles who are Muslims, something they never bothered to find out earlier", says Dikshit Patel, a videographer from the city. Muslims comprise 15.3 per cent of the city's population and have been long-standing residents of the city. Many are well-established merchants, traders and businessmen. Within the walled city the two communities have lived cheek by jowl in areas like Kalupur and Daryapur, giving rise to communal friction at times. But, notwithstanding such conflict, there has been little opportunity to feign ignorance of the other. The above mentioned queries of children thus strike a note of distancing and separation, uncharacteristic of this old city.

Again, several observers have mentioned that Muslim majority areas, especially in the newer parts of the city, like Juhapura, Tandalja, for instance, have been dubbed as 'mini-Pakistan'.[2] These areas, overwhelmingly minority inhabited, have developed as a result of overt ghettoization of the population. Recurrent communal strife from the mid-1980s to mid-1990s, including the rioting that occurred in 1993 after the Babri Masjid demolition, drove the minorities into these ghettos in search of security. The displacement of minorities from mixed localities and their congregation in large, overcrowded and relatively poor circumstances, has turned these localities in the mind of outsider Hindus into 'an anonymous mass'.[3] Several factors have contributed to this segregated social existence of communities. But, the net result has been a sense of separation, apprehension and mistrust, which has created the conditions of possibility of the 'will to hate' and spurred the continuing communal violence in the state after Godhra.

Communal violence is not new to Ahmedabad or Gujarat but it had hardly ever been of this 'ethnic cleansing' or pogrom dimension. What is specific to this latest phase is the one-sided nature of the violence, the planned way in which retribution was executed and the active collusion of the state in the process. In order to understand how communal violence acquired the dimension of a pogrom or ethnic cleansing, 'will to hate' serves as an index. Foucault, in his analytics of 'bio-power', refers back to the Sophists of the early Greek civilization. The displacement of the poetic discourse of the Sophists by the rise of theory and the Platonic 'will to truth' coincides with the institutionalization of the state.[4] To interrogate the totalization of the 'will to know', Foucault invokes the prior state of knowing. It is a means to examine "the beginnings of the totalizing ordering of things".[5] Similarly, in the Gujarat case, I introduce the notion of 'will to hate' as the normalized situation of communal polarization as it prevails presently. But, the thrust of this paper is directed to understand how this state of affairs came to be. The rest of the paper is divided into two parts. The first chronicles the 'present' starting with the Godhra incident paying special attention to role of rumours and the new media, globalization of Hindutva, the state's role, economic decimation of the minorities and the targeting of women and children.

Godhra and After

On 27 February 2002, early in the morning, the Sabarmati Express arrived at Godhra station, about five hours late. Many of the passengers were *kar sevaks* who had gone for the *shilanyas* to Ayodhya and were returning home. Some of the passengers who had disembarked got into an altercation with food vendors on the platform about payment. Apparently, some of the *kar sevaks* misbehaved with passengers of the minority community on the platform too. As the train was pulling out of the station and there were many passengers who had not been able to get in, the train was stopped before it had left the platform. After a few minutes it resumed its journey but was again halted by the pulling of the emergency chain barely a kilometre from the station at Signal Faliya. Here, a mob of 2,000, mostly Ghanchi Muslims from the surrounding Signal Faliya slums, attacked the train with stones and fire bombs. The target of their attack seems to have been coaches S-6 and S-5. But, while the former coach was completely burnt, the latter was not so badly damaged. Along with the coach, 58 passengers, including 26 women, 12 children and 20 men, perished. The Ganchis are said to have attacked the train on being informed by their compatriots on the platform that *kar sevaks* had misbehaved with vendors of their community and on the rumoured abduction of a Muslim women.[6]

The attack seems to have been spontaneous with little or no pre-planning. The two damaged bogies were detached at Godhra and the train continued on its journey at 12.40 p.m. Meanwhile, with the arrival of the police, district authorities and the fire fighters, the fire could be dowsed. All the dead bodies, except five local passengers, were sent to the Civil Hospital at Sola, Ahmedabad, for postmortem. The arrival of the bodies in Ahmedabad served to inflame passions. The unfortunate and ghastly incident was widely broadcast in the national print and electronic media and in the Gujarati language press and cable channels. The Gujarati press, long known for its partisanship, was soon engaged in inflammatory reporting. For instance, the newspaper *Sandhesh* reported on 1st March that two Hindu women were abducted from the train, gangraped, mutilated by cutting off their private parts and their dead bodies dumped in Kalol near Godhra. The story had been filed without cross-checking the facts with the police or government authorities and was entirely false as later police investigations revealed. But, its circulation had done the damage and raised Hindu retributory passions to a fever pitch.[7]

The Baroda edition of *Gujarat Samachar* reported on its first page on 28th February that three or four young girls had been kidnapped without attributing any source. On page 10, on the same day, it carried a report that the VHP leader Kaushik Patel had said that 10 girls had been abducted. This information was neither cross-checked nor any details were given. Another report on page 2 of the same day's edition carried an eyewitness account by one Hetalben, travelling by the fateful train. She said that "young girls from Amaralwadi travelling with us are lost".[8] All these unsubstantiated reports not only fuelled Hindu retributory desires but also incited retaliatory violence.

However, it is significant to note that while such inflammatory reporting is actionable in law and comprises a cognizable offence, yet the state government did not make any effort to prosecute the erring newspapers. Instead, as the newspapers pandered to the inclination of the majority community, it was able to enhance its credibility. So much so that a report on the media's role maintains that, "over the past months of violence people's own experience in their neighbourhood as well as reports in the national media are often *relied on less* than Sandesh's reports" (emphasis added).[9] Even as Chief Minister Narendra Modi complained against the national press and electronic media for partisan and one-sided depiction of events, it did nothing against the local media. In some areas, Star TV was blacked out for a brief period and some local cable TV channels, which were broadcasting the carnage in Ahmedabad to incite residents to participate, were banned for some time.[10]

The bodies sent for postmortem from Godhra to the Civil Hospital, Sola, Ahmedabad, arrived there at around 10.30 p.m. But, the news had already been broadcast over the radio and led to a huge incensed crowd gathering at the hospital. The display of the charred bodies and body parts aggravated passions. Retaliatory slogans like "*khoon ka badla khoon*" were raised at the hospital and were printed the following morning as newspaper headlines (in *Sandesh,* for instance).[11] Earlier, in the day, the Vishwa Hindu Parishad (VHP) had called for a bandh on 28th February. This was supported by the state government. The stage had been set for the carnage and bloodletting that was to follow.

The next day mobs went on the rampage looting, burning, destroying the goods of the minority community. But, these retaliatory acts were targeted specifically, planned and carried out with precision by practised groups. Clearly, all mobs had a core of adept volunteers acting like a militia force of the VHP. As Barkha Dutt of NDTV reported, there was nothing spontaneous in every seventh shop being gutted. The pogrom was well planned. Truckloads of LPG cylinders were used to set fire to houses and business enterprises. Rags were dipped in kerosene and flung at minorities inhabited residential complexes, as were fire bombs, shops and buildings were burnt by using LPG cylinders as explosives. The question obviously arises that while citizens had to wait their turn for LPG cylinders, from where did truckloads of these scarce items appear?

Violence in the old city of Ahmedabad has a pattern of reciprocal brickbatting, throwing fire rags among neighbouring housing societies and stabbings. But, after Godhra, mobs of five to 5,000 people got together and went on the rampage. They were bent on burning, looting, killing and destroying property. Their prime targets were the localities, which had come up outside the walled city like Juhapura, Vejalpur, Paldi, Vastrapur, Naroda Patiya, Bapunagar. Here, the residences as well as the business establishments of the minority community were sought and destroyed. In the mobs people had lists of addresses as well as names of shops and establishments which were owned by the minority community. Consequently, a large number of business establishments, including shops, hotels and offices, which were not directly identified with the minority community, either by their name, or were co-owned with Hindu partners, or had sleeping partners from among them, were identified and systematically set ablaze. In all this the state machinery's complicity and VHP role have become well known.

In an interview with journalist Sheela Bhat, the 96-year-old chairman of the Gujarat unit of VHP has clearly stated that the list of shops and business establishments to be attacked were drawn up on 28th February morning. A highly respected Gujarati litterateur and scholar of the *Mahabharat,* Prof. Keshavram Kashirarn Shastri said, "In the morning we sat down and prepared the list. We were not prepared in advance". Asked why they did it, Prof. Shastri replied, "It had to be done, it had to be done. We don't like it but we are terribly angry. Lust and anger are blind". About the rioters he mentioned them as '*kelvayela stindu chokra*' (well bred Hindu boys). While attributing the violence to a 'frenzy' he added about non-violence, "These things (non-violence) look good in the *shastras.* Our boys were charged because in Godhra women and children were burnt alive. The crowd was spontaneous. All of them were not VHP people. The Waghri community (a Scheduled Caste) didn't even know the victims of Godhra, but they have done an amazing job! They are not our members. In villages all these people who were angry are not our people.

They are angry because Hindutva was attacked.[12] This is an outburst—a tremendous outburst—that will be difficult to roll back". From this interview of an elderly and educated VHP leader we obtain some clues of the particularity of pogrom participation. Firstly, it was largely the middle class educated youth who were incited by the BJP local leaders and the saffronites to lead the rampage. These were no illiterate, lumpen or destitute mobs.

It is being made out to be that they were all enraged by the Godhra atrocity and engaged in spontaneous vandalism. If it had been so why was it necessary to egg them on by the saffronites? Also how did the lists of requisite victims reach them? Are electoral lists so readily available? Finally, why were the excesses promoted knowing full well that their effects were likely to be disastrous for the cohesion of the society? For when neighbours turn predators and engage in venting their hate, it tears asunder the social fabric which has been built over time. In Gujarat, while the communal faultlines had been visible since 1969, segregation has now reached the point of exclusion. Even as I write, renewed violence and arson in Ahmedabad is all about preventing the refugees from returning to their homes.[13] As Prof. Shastri mentions that the violent outburst would be difficult to 'roll back', it is increasingly evident that there is not even the desire for 'roll back'.

Government complicity and direction in the pogrom is manifest from several sources. The rioters were marshalled and brought in luxury buses. The police and civil administration were asked to turn a blind eye on vandalism and murder. At a meeting of senior officers and the political leadership on the evening of 27th February, officers were told to do nothing "which would hurt Hindu sentiments".[14] That the police had been tipped off not to harm the Hindus was even public knowledge scrawled on, for instance, the charred walls of a burnt madarasa in Sundaraninagar, "*Yeh andar ki baat hai, police hamarey saath hai*".[15] Note the language of this message. It is a play on an advertisement caption for a well-known brand of undergarments (Lux) and epitomises the nexus of consumption with violence. But far more sinister had been the attempt at 'ethnic mapping' attempted by the state government. Early in February 1999, the Director of Police (Intelligence), P.B. Upadhyaya had sent a confidential circular to all Police Commissioners and district police officers to provide details of existing Muslim organizations including names and addresses of their office bearers, and also of Muslims participating in certain religious activities. This secret circular and a similar one on Christians was challenged in the Gujarat High Court and revoked a month later. But during the month information was already collected. Later a market survey organization, which visited various establishments to collect data on ownership production, sales and number of employees, etc., is suspected to have been clandestinely involved in an ethnic mapping exercise.[16]

The Gujarati press was also privy to this kind of information. It has been alleged that about eight months ago *Sandesh* published an article which listed the names of establishments which bore secular names but were owned by Muslims.

The way the police stood by and watched or joined in the carnage in various parts of Gujarat and Ahmedabad, can hardly absolve the state government of its partisanship. It not only allowed the mobs to run amuck but also abrogated its constitutional responsibility by not protecting the life and property of politicians like Ahsan Jafri (Congress ex-MLA) at the Gulbarg Apartments in Chamanpuria, or the property of Justice Qadri, a sitting High Court judge at Vastrapur.

The response of the police and administration has raised questions of the communalization or saffronization of the rank and file. The lower ranks of the administration or the police force include very few Muslims or Dalits. Lack of diversity in their ranks has also made them prone to the communalization of public sensibility. It is this which may have prompted the

Police Commissioner of Ahmedabad, P.C. Pande to acknowledge that the police may not have been above the bias of the local populace.

Another factor, which may have contributed to the large scale brutal violence, is the state's fashioning of the incidents as a surrogate war with Pakistan. The Godhra incident immediately evoked a response from Chief Minister, Narendra Modi, that it was a pre-planned, ISI-sponsored attack. Union Home Minister L.K. Advani echoed the message in his statement too. This equated the Ghanchi Muslims of Signal Falia with Pakistanis. As the State Health Minister Ashok Bhatt said on 27th February at Godhra, "Godhra has a notorious reputation ... We suspect that many Pakistanis live here illegally."[17] In Ahmedabad, areas which had large Muslim communities came to be known as 'mini-Pakistan'. A swift and easy conflation of all Muslims as Pakistanis enabled the mobs to wreak such impersonal violence. For once they became Pakistanis, they became enemies of the nation and hence had to be eliminated. The supplanting of other identities like friends, neighbours or business partners, by that of the national enemy or even international enemy as Islamic terrorists, facilitated large-scale killing and destruction of the minorities. For the pogrom took on the character of an internal war. The ratification of the international community's war against terrorism could well have influenced the NRI sponsors of the VHP and BJP in Gujarat. This may also have facilitated the process of identification of Muslims with terrorists—a most unfortunate conflation.

After the postmortem, when the bodies of the Godhra victims were being carried in a huge funeral procession in Ahmedabad on 28th February, the mob went on the rampage. As the procession wound its way through the city, parts of the procession went off into roads and lanes where Muslims resided and attacked them indiscriminately, and started killing, stabbing, burning and looting. Large numbers of middle class men and women joined in the carnage, burning shops, houses, vehicles and looting shops. The looting, which took place in Ahmedabad, especially in the 'posh' localities, west of the Sabarmati river, were indulged in by the well-to-do middle class. Shobha De, in her open letter to the Gujarat Chief Minister, mentions about a woman in a red lancer who was busy carting goods to her car from a well-known city shop. Or again this woman who went into a shoe shop while her husband waited in the car. The shoes she initially brought out did not fit her husband, so she went back to change them. People used their mobile phones to send SMS messages about the nature of goods available for looting and where! Amoral greed and the overwhelming desire to consume seems to have overcome the middle class population in Gujarat.[18]

The violence soon spread to Baroda, Rajkot, Bhavnagar and in the neighbouring villages of Mehsana, Banaskantha, Panchmahal, Anand and Sabarkantha districts. In Baroda, where stray stabbings had occurred on 27th evening, large-scale attacks began the next day at the Wadi area. These too were often fuelled by rumours of impending attacks by Muslims. In Sardarpura village of Mehsana district, some 23 persons were burnt alive in a house. Residents from Rajkot sent bangles to Bhavnagar for not initially joining in the fray of Muslim baiting.

Violence in communal situations is often said to be perpetrated by 'outsiders' and anti-social elements. In the Gujarat situation, even the pretense of this separation has been dropped. Victims and survivors of the violence have identified the killers and arsonists but are being thwarted from filing FIRs with names. Many of the perpetrators were neighbours or people known to the victims with whom they apparently had good relations. What has bewildered and horrified them has been the familiar turning fatal. As a woman in Baroda's Qureshi Jamaat Khaana Camp mentioned, "these were boys who grew up in front of us".[19]

The targeting of women and children has invoked the epithet of 'ethnic cleansing' and 'genocide'. Even if these charges are exaggerated, the desire to drive out Muslims and even to physically rid some neighbourhoods of them, seems to have been at work in this violence. In one of the worst bit areas of Ahmedabad, Narodiya Patia, 84 persons were killed by a 15,000 strong mob on 28th February.

New Media and the Old

Even as the Gujarati press and electronic media served to aggravate passions, what distinguished these riots were the use of the new media to communicate and incite violence. Three sources of communication aided in the swift relaying of information. Local cable TV networks cashed in on the mood and broadcast the violence, looting and arson in their localities. These images had a demonstration effect and also fuelled apprehensions of retributory strikes by the minority.

SMS messages on the mobile phones were widely used to transmit rumours and hearsay. This had a spiralling effect on violence. Moreover, SMS messages or mobile phone calls were widely used to alert people of excellent looting opportunities, or what was available where!

E-mail messages left on the computer were also widely used to convey desperate situations, as well as other messages. When people were confined because of the curfew, e-mail messages were used to communicate. Before she perished with her father Ahsan Jafri, Congress ex-MLA, at Gulmarg Society, his daughter was able to send an e-mail message describing the attack on their house.

Use of communication medium in such a big way, amply indicates that the communal violence in Gujarat was neither confined to traditional neighbourhoods nor among the slum dwellers in the city. There was a systematic effort to attack the Muslim middle class and to decimate them physically and economically. In this, rumours and rumour-like transmissions like the reports in the *Sandesh* had a major role to play. Three kinds of rumours were potent in aggravating the situation. That women of the community were abducted, killed or violated. In such situations of communal violence women explicitly become emblematic of the community's honour. Again, rumours or hearsay of the desecration of places of worship served as grave incitement. Also news of an impending attack by the other community galvanized retributory action. All these three types of rumours were liberally used to mobilize the majority community during the Gujarat violence.

Economic Dislocation

A leaflet circulated in Ahmedabad by the VHP mentions: "Economic boycott is the only solution! The anti-national elements use the money earned from the Hindus to destroy us...! The way to break the backbone of these elements is: An economic non-cooperation movement.... Such strict economic boycott will throttle these elements! It will break their backbone! Then it will be difficult for them to live in any corner of this country..."[20] Similar leaflets were not only distributed in many of the riot-affected areas in Ahmedabad but also in Baroda, Kalol near Godhra and other places.

In all these leaflets, the tenor is that of separation and segregation. As if a partition of the mind had already taken place and that of space was a matter of course. Economic boycott, along with social and cultural boycott, were the means to enforce it. Clearly, the sense of separation among the two communities has grown to an extent where the other community has become an object of hate.

The leaflets speak of breaking the 'backbone' of the minority, so that they can neither recover nor return to their original homes. By destroying the businesses and enterprises, the VHP and other constituents of the saffron brigade have not only destroyed homes but also sources of livelihood or economic sustenance. In some areas like Gomtipur, the displaced residents have not been welcomed back. Areas vacated during the carnage are sought to be appropriated by the people of the locality or builders.

Narratives of Communal Polarization

The events after Godhra have caused considerable reflection and soul searching among a section of the Gujarati intelligentsia to understand and explain why the communal violence was so virulent, widespread, engulfing the middle class, thereby transforming an ostensibly non-violent, commercially motivated people from Gandhi's land into these marauding mobs? Several explanations have emerged in this regard. For instance, Achyut Yagnik has argued, that it is the changing self-perception of 'Bhadra Gujarat' as contrasted to 'Aam Gujarat' that has stoked the violence.[21] In the face of an incipient transfer of power from the 'ujaliat' (upper castes) to the 'pachhat' (backward castes) in the wake of the KHAM strategy of the Congress government in the 1980s, when backward caste reservation was extended in government jobs, this reactive aggression has crystallized and displaced on to differences of religion. 'Savarna' unity has been over the last decade been transformed into Hindu unity through VHP and BJP's mobilization. The latter have systematically over the last decade sought to unite the Hindus against difference, whether it be against the Christian tribals or more recently against the Muslims.

On the other hand, Shreekant Sambrani considers the amoral accumulation of wealth in the shadows of legality, decline of the Protestant/Vaishnav/Jain work ethics giving rise to the 'chal se' attitude. This has promoted an attitude to consumption, which is sought to be fulfilled by the emergent middle class section with scant regard to the legality of the means. Hence financial speculation and shadowy entrepreneurship has overshadowed industrial enterprises.[22] Moreover, with the police undermining their authority as law enforcers through complicity with the illicit trade in liquor in the 'prohibition' state, the rampaging mobs disregarded the police with impunity. Sometimes, the police joined with the mobs rather than thwarting their action. This waning of the work ethic and loss of faith in the police provided an impetus to communal aggression and violence against the Muslims in general and the well-to-do Muslims in particular.

Jan Breman, a long-standing analyst of Gujarat and more specifically Ahmedabad, has remarked on how the closing down of many textile mills in the city has led to a shrinkage of secular social space.[23] According to him, the Majoor Mahajan as the leading trade union of the textile workers afforded a space for secular interaction of workers. With the drastic reduction of the textile workforce, the leading trade union has also lost its significance. This has led to greater informalization of the labour force which because of the oppressive conditions of work are easily prone to ethnic fragmentation.

From the above narratives it is evident that the conditions for communal animosity had been created over a period of time over the last one decade. But, these were ultimately capitalized on by the BJP and VHP to serve their ends. The campaign by the Sangh Parivar against minorities like Christians and Muslims culminated in the distribution of *trishuls* which effected a militarization of the campaign. It is this which might have given rise to the widespread violence in the aftermath of Godhra. The 'will to hate' has become the nomenclature of politics in one of India's most industrially advanced state. An indication that hate is not necessarily a primordial mode of distinction but a modern one as well.

Notes

1. Debashis Bhattacharyya, 'Identity goes under the razor to protect body from knife', *The Telegraph,* 4 March, 2002, p. 1.
2. Manu Joseph, 'Body of evidence', *The Outlook,* 6 May, 2002, p. 13; Jan Breman, 'Communal upheaval as resurgence of Social Darwinism', *Economic and Political Weekly,* 37, 16, 20-26 April, pp. 1485-88.

3. Breman, *ibid.*, p. 1487.
4. H.L. Dreyfus and P. Rabinow, *Michel Foucault: Beyond Structuralism and Hermeneuties,* Sussex, The Harvester Press, 1986, p. 201.
5. *Ibid.*, p. 203.
6. 'An Independent Fact Finding Mission', *Gujarat Carnage 2002: A Report to the Nation,* April, 2002. (The Mission comprised of Dr. Kamal Mitra Chenoy, S.P. Shukla, K.S. Subramanian and Achin Vinaik), p. 4.
7. *Ibid.*
8. PUCL Vadodara and Shanti Abhiyan, Baroda, *The Role of Newspapers during the Gujarat Carnage: A Brief Analysis for the period February 28 to March 24, 2002*, p. 6.
9. *Ibid.*
10. Independent Fact Finding Mission, *op. cit.*, p. 9.
11. PUCL, Baroda and Shanti Abhiyan, *op. cit.*, p. 2.
12. Sheela Bhatt, 'VHP Leader's Startling Revelation', *Mainstream,* 16 March, 2002, p.5.
13. Basant Rawat, 'Hounded come home to carnage', *The Telegraph,* 6 May, 2002, p. 1.
14. 'Independent Fact Finding Mission', *op. cit.*, p. 13.
15. SAHMAT, *Genocide in Ahmedabad,* March, 2002, the preliminary report as published in *Anya Swar/Other Voice,* March, 2002, p. 218.
16. *Ibid.*, p. 14.
17. Independent Fact Finding Mission, *op. cit.*, p. 10.
18. Shobha De, 'Open letter to the Gujarat CM', *Sunday Times of India,* 10 March, 2002.
19. PUCL Vadodara and Shanti Abhiyan, *Women's Perspectives on the Violence in Gujarat,* March 2002.
20. A VHP leaflet in Gujarati, translated and appended to the Independent Fact Finding Mission's Report, *op. cit.*, p. 35.
21. Achyut Yagnik and Suchitra Sheth, 'Whither Gujarat? Violence and After', *Economic and Political Weekly,* 16 March, 2002, pp. 1010-11.
22. Shreekant Sambrani, 'Gujarat's burning train: India's inferno', *Economic and Political Weekly,* 6 April, 2002, pp. 1308-09.
23. Breman, *op. cit.*

Contributors

Anjan Ghosh is Fellow at the Centre for Studies in Social Sciences, Kolkata.

Vinod K. Jairath is Reader in the Department of Sociology at the University of Hyderabad, Hyderabad.

Paramjit S. Judge is Professor of Sociology at Guru Nanak Dev University, Amritsar.

M.N. Karna is former Professor of Sociology at the North-Eastern Hill University, Shillong.

Kulwinder Kaur is Research Associate in the Department of Sociology at the University of Delhi, Delhi.

S.K. Nanda teaches Sociology in the Department of Agricultural Production and Rural Development at the North-Eastern Hill University, Tura Campus.

T.K. Oommen is former Professor of Sociology, Jawaharlal Nehru University, New Delhi.

Rowena Robinson teaches Sociology at the Indian Institute of Technology, Mumbai.

N. Sudhakar Rao is Professor of Sociology at the Assam University, Silchar.

Virginius Xaxa is Professor of Sociology at the University of Delhi, Delhi.

Index